The Natural Form of Man
The Basic Practices and Beliefs of Islam

THE NATURAL FORM OF MAN

THE BASIC PRACTICES AND BELIEFS OF ISLAM

Abdalhaqq Bewley

TA-HA PUBLISHERS LTD

The Natural Form of Man

© Abdalhaqq Bewley 1429 AH/ 2008 CE

First Published as Islam, its Basic Practices and Beliefs, by Ta-Ha Publishers Ltd. in January 2008

This edition published in 1437AH/March 2016

Published by: Ta-Ha Publishers Ltd.

Unit 4, The Windsor Centre

Windsor Grove

West Norwood

SE27 9NT

United Kingdom

Website: www.tahapublishers.com

E-mail: sales@tahapublishers.com

Written by: Abdalhaqq Bewley

Edited and typeset by: Abdassamad Clarke

A catalogue record of this book is available from the British Library.

ISBN-13: 978-1-84200-158-5

Printed and bound by Imak Ofset

Contents

IN THE NAME OF ALLAH, THE ALL-MERCIFUL, THE MOST MERCIFUL

Introduction

Every baby born is an expression of absolute purity. Anyone who has been present at a birth must acknowledge this. Each new birth is a bursting out of life itself. Every baby is a container for the re-emergence of raw life-energy – unadulterated, undifferentiated. However, this container has a definite form and comes into a specific environment. Each baby has genetic coding determining its physical shape and temperamental balance and each baby is born into surroundings of a particular nature both physical and emotional. These circumstances, together with the chain of events that make up its early life, bring about the individualisation of the new child. They combine together to make the child, in its own unique way, begin to feel itself separate from its own surroundings. Some receive affirmation and satisfaction and so view the world as a friendly, warm, safe place; others are negated and denied and so experience the world as hostile, alien and threatening; and between these two are millions of possibilities and variations different for each child. On the other hand, the kinds of human situations confronted by the child are quite limited and predictable, just as its own specific temperament is of a given type, so that the end result is a being both in every case unique and yet at the same time falling within a clearly recognisable category, in just the way that, while no two individuals are sick in exactly the same way, the particular illness they are both suffering from can still be diagnosed.

At a certain point, after roughly two years, a picture built up of all the various elements mentioned above takes on a more or less definite shape and the child says, "This is me!" But this "me" is, in fact, by no means solid, but changing from one minute to the next, although it is established enough as a shape to be claimed as an identity. It is vitally important, however, to realise that this "identity" has no real existence in an absolute sense. What has happened is that the pure life energy and undifferentiated consciousness of the newborn baby have, over a period of time and through exposure to a particular environment and together with its innate genetic coding, identified in a particular way with its body-container and become limited and individualised in it.

Through the process of existing, the child has acquired a more or less fixed image of itself which it calls "me", completely losing sight of the unconstrained, undefined, pure life-energy which was its birthright. This assumed identity is accidental, made up out of contingent circumstances and passing time. Given a different environment, a child would adopt a different self-form. The true reality of the child lies in the pure life energy and undifferentiated consciousness it starts with, not the limited and constricted self-picture it later develops.

This circumstantially constructed, arbitrarily imposed first self-image now becomes for us the basis of all our future dealings with ourselves and with the world which surrounds us. It dictates to us the pattern of our life which is, from now on, spent preserving and perpetuating the existence of this assumed identity we have inextricably associated ourselves with. As far as we are concerned, it is what we are. However, just look at any two year-old and you will find a very unbridled raw-edged being: wilful, autocratic, demanding, easily angered, often destructive, attention-seeking, extremely selfish – in a word, monstrous!

In its naked form this "self" is obviously not acceptable, but gradually we learn by experience to negotiate with existence. We find out how much we can get away with, what needs to be honed down, what we can express and what we must hold back, what brings about desired reactions and so on. In other words, we try to find a balance between the raw material of our acquired self-picture, to which we have given absolute reality, and the hampering social environment in which we find ourselves, where total "self" expression is not permissible or possible. In this way, our original self-picture becomes covered over layer upon layer according to the demands of different life situations. But our lives continue to be the playing-out of that first patterning, more and more refined and in an ever larger arena.

In cases where a completely free rein is given to the inclinations of the primary self-image, the individual will return to his infantile form as in the case of the reclusive billionaire Howard Hughes who reverted absolutely to a tyrannical infant, concerned only with the gratification of his capricious whims and unbounded appetites. It also occurs to some extent in senility when an old person loses grip on the cover-up which has been so successfully maintained for so many years. This is the inevitable description of one who has given absolute reality to his acquired self-picture. If this were all that there was, we would have no other option than to be slaves to our own self-imposed identities; our lives would be spent hopelessly trying to assuage the appetites and gratify the desires of a two year-old child. And this is in the fact the lot of an increasingly large proportion of the human race.

However, as we saw earlier, this assumed self-image is not the whole picture. The reality of the self stretches beyond it, before it, to that life energy which preceded it and provided the dynamic for its formation. You can only escape a hopelessly trapped, self-destructive existence taken up in vain pursuit of endlessly elusive gratification of the infantile self-form by consciously determining to refuse to bow to its claim of absolute reality and by consciously and repeatedly acknowledging the life-force which permitted its existence.

If you look about you at the phenomena of existence in the outside world or inside yourself at the workings of your own body, you will find clearly discernible laws at work, holding everything in harmony and balance. In the vastness of the galaxies and the overwhelming beauty of the stars in their constellations with their patterns and movement. In the solar system and the wonderful way that the planets keep to their orbits held by an unbelievably intricate system of forces. In the earth's atmosphere and how it provides exactly the right conditions for the life on its surface. In the climates and how they preserve the animal and vegetable life in their different zones. In the forest and the desert and how each is a delicately balanced ecological system providing everything necessary for its continued existence. In the separate organisms, each with its own inexplicable breathtaking beauty and its own perfectly balanced cycle of growth and decay. In our own bodies with their perfect co-ordination. With the senses, each with its own field of perception. With the digestive system and its extraction of what is beneficial and its rejection of what is superfluous. With the brain and its ability to store information and release it in the right situation. With the natural healing process and the way the body naturally sets right any disruption of its equilibrium. The examples are endless, but the indications are quite clear. Whether you look at the whole universe or a particular system or a single organism or the smallest subatomic particle, it is abundantly apparent that there is a universal law at work tending to order and balance in every situation.

Only in the case of human beings does there appear to be a contradiction of this harmony. They rush about, on, above and underneath the surface of the earth, wreaking havoc at will, upsetting the natural balance, slaughtering vast numbers of other creatures, ransacking natural resources, polluting beyond use great areas of the globe, turning on each other with an unprecedented fury and so on *ad nauseam*. And it is happening more now than at any previous time and with apparently ever-increasing ferocity and velocity. The reason for this is that the vast majority of the human species are only concerned with the entirely self-centred gratification of the appetites of the wilful infant they carry untamed inside them in the mistaken belief that this is all that there is. They are quite frankly completely out of control.

This unruly self, however, is not the only facet of the human being and every person has another instrument with which to approach existence – the enlightened faculty of the intellect. The intellect is the means by which the grip of man's self-imposed tyranny can begin to be loosened. Intellect in this context does not designate so much the capacity of collecting, storing, and reproducing information common to every human being, but rather the capacity of seeing situations for what they really are, the faculty of clear discrimination between what is harmful and what is beneficial. It is by the intellect that we are able to perceive the universal law of balance and harmony working in the universe and that we ourselves are apparently, for the most part, at variance with it. It is the intellect that enables us to see that we are more than our infantile self-form and that we have a part to play in the whole scheme of things beyond the mere gratification of our sensual appetites.

When you look out into the creation, you cannot fail to see that every creature, every atom even, has a definite part to play in the creational process. The interdependence and mutual reliance of particles, cells, organisms, systems, is now an established fact recognised in every field of scientific research. This means that the form of a thing does not stop at its physical outline but extends well beyond it into the environment surrounding it. For instance, a planet is more than a mass floating in space. It produces and affects the intricate force fields of all the other bodies in the same system. The same applies to everything in existence, whatever its nature, whatever its size.

We can take the example of a cat. You might pick up the physical form of a cat and say, "This is a cat." But if you reflect for a minute, you will find that "catness" goes far beyond the animal body you are holding. As much a part of a cat as its whiskers and tail are its careful washing and grooming, its meticulous eating habits, the way it naturally hides its excreta, the distinctive manner in which it moves, sits and lies, its purring when contented, the way it arches its back when threatened, with its fur standing on end, its motionless lying in wait when hunting, the way it pounces and plays with its prey. All these and other things are as essential to the being of a cat as its physical form. If they are lacking, it is defective as a cat. Also clear, from reflecting on the form of the cat, is the part it plays in upholding the natural balance by its activity of hunting mice and other small creatures, thus helping towards sustaining the harmony of the whole universe.

Any other creature would in fact serve equally well as an example. The point is that every creature has a natural form that extends beyond its physical outline into the zone of behaviour. Every creature also has a clear function in the process of existence by which it plays its own unique and indispensable part in maintaining the harmony and balance within its own sphere and, by extension, in the whole universe. And since this is true for everything in existence, it must be that it is true for human beings as well. It must be that we too have a particular behaviour-form, that we too have a specific function to fulfil in the creational process.

How is it then that everything seems inherently to know its form and function except human beings who are clearly extremely confused on both counts? It seems that we have gone outside the limits of our form and lost touch with it and that we have certainly lost any clear idea of what our function should be. If this were not the case, there would be the same ecological balance in the human zone as there is in every other sphere of existence and it is plain to see that there is not. So what is our natural pattern? What is our role? How can we find out?

As we have noted, wherever you look in the universe you

inevitably find a natural order and balance and everything plays its part in upholding it. It is a dynamic, fluid order where there is continual movement and consequent continual re-adjustment of internal and external forces to keep the status quo. In all of this only man and what he makes appear strident and discordant. Another thing that is quite clear when you look at natural phenomena is that everything is determined; there is no choice involved. A star has no option but to behave the way it does. The planets have no choice as to their orbit. The same applies in the mineral, vegetable and animal worlds on the earth's surface. A daffodil cannot become a rose. A donkey cannot change into a horse.

Each creature is limited and defined by what it is, to being what it is. And it is by every creature and form being what it is that the universal balance is maintained. Everything by its nature both submits to the universal order and plays its own part in preserving it and it is only in the case of man that there appears to be an exception to this rule. It is in this apparent contradiction that the clear indication of our role in existence lies.

Since it is quite clear that there is nothing "haphazard" in existence, a statement borne out by what we have discussed, and demonstrated beyond doubt by all the recent research in every branch of scientific learning, which shows in every case how minutely each form, organism, particle affects the entire environment, it is absolutely inconceivable that in the case of man the universal law is broken, that suddenly "it all went wrong". On the contrary, it is precisely our ability to go against the natural order of things that contains the clue to the purpose of human existence. Our role in existence lies in the fact that we are able to choose to recognise, submit to, and play our part in preserving the natural order and balance apparent in the universe, or on the other hand, to go against it and disrupt it.

From this, it is quite obvious that there is great difference between human beings and all other forms of existence. Every other thing perfectly fulfils its appointed role, aware of its own limited function and environment. This is the case from the densest mineral life to the highest animal life, from the smallest particle to the largest mass. Between man and all other animals there is as great a leap as between animals and vegetable life or even greater. This is because the human species possesses speech – we are language creatures.

A human being is as prepared by his form for talking as a bird is for flying or a fish for swimming. Modern research has shown that language is not something acquired but rather that linguistic capacity is genetically inherent in a child and emerges gradually. It is this innate linguistic ability, this power to name, to describe, to give expression to intellectual perception, that gives the human species mastery over other creatures. Other creatures are outward and their function is outward. Language is an inward capacity and gives us inwardness and the possibility of reflection and concentration and inner awareness not possessed by any other creature.

It also gives us the ability, and at the same time demonstrates our capacity, to know not only our own environment but also the totality of existence. By our capacity for language, we are able to read the universe, to see within ourselves and in what surrounds us the universal order and balance and to know that we ourselves are inseparably a part of it. We are able to reflect on our own essential nature and by doing so to reach the unavoidable conclusion that all phenomena manifest one single reality, that all the disparate yet inter-connected and balanced elements that make up the universe are clear indications that point to a single source from which everything emanates and to which everything will inevitably return.

Apart from the case of man, it is quite apparent that everything submits involuntarily and unconsciously, just by being what it is, to the universal order manifest in existence, or we could say by extension, to the Divine Reality which it indicates. Everything also, each thing in its own unique way, contributes to the upholding of the balance and is itself, in itself, an indication of its Creator/Source – in the same way that any artefact indicates the person who made it.

It is this activity of submission and participation in the unfolding of existence, this acknowledgement, even if unconscious, of the source of existence, that constitutes real worship. At this point you must jettison any concept you may previously have held of worship being connected to "religion". Worship is organic, inevitable. It is an integral part of all existence. By fulfilling its natural function for which it is perfectly adapted, every creature is at the same time performing an act of worship and playing its own part in manifesting and indicating the One Reality. All things, in spite of the diversity of their different forms and activities, have this one thing in common. This is the common denominator in existence. This is the common purpose.

Now we come back to the human species, to ourselves. By use of the intellect, we must arrive at the conclusion that what is true for everything else in the universe must also be true for us, since we are an inseparable part of the whole. Just as the basic function of everything in the universe is unconscious worship, so worship must also be the keynote of our own existence but in our case it will be conscious.

Whereas everything else acknowledges its Creator outwardly by its natural unconscious submission to the way things are, we by our faculty of inward articulation, have the capacity of both outward submission to, and also inner awareness of, the one reality. This then is our purpose, our reason for being here, and also what defines our outward form – that we both outwardly conform to the natural boundaries imposed on us by the form which we have been given and that we inwardly realise our capacity for decoding what we see around us and accept that existence is what it is, a generous and compassionate outpouring, the self-manifestation of the essence of the One God, the Lord of the heavens and the earth and everything between them.

These boundaries delineating the natural form of the human

being, showing what it is to be a human creature, have always been available to people, accepted by some, rejected by others, together with the knowledge of the true picture of existence. All creatures except man have their form indelibly stamped in them so that they have no need of external stimuli to bring them out of them. But in our case, the tendency is to go beyond the bounds. We have to choose to be human. We have to choose the form that is in reality our true nature. It is very important to grasp this. Even though we have to learn what it is to be truly human, all we are doing is removing ignorance and uncovering what is in fact our organic natural pattern.

What this means is that what is generally called morality is not something imposed on man out of social convenience, but something that is inherent in us and required by our form for the proper functioning of the human social nexus. In illustration of this: there is a type of goose that is naturally monogamous. Once it has chosen its mate, it remains with it until one or the other of them dies. Then the survivor can only mate with another whose own mate has also died. This is not brought about by some elder goose preaching that anything other than monogamy is forbidden for such geese! It is a natural patterning coming from within them and appearing in a social context. The unlicensed behaviour, the unrestricted giving way to the infantile appetites, which is the present hallmark of the human situation, is in fact unnatural. It constitutes a covering-up of the simple moral order that is the true reality of human society. Morality is the organic result of a natural patterning allowed to express itself in the social sphere.

We have noted that every creature knows its form and it is not in the evidently compassionate nature of existence that we, the human species, should alone be left with no way to know the form we should take on to truly fulfil our humanness and of course the simple fact is that we have not been neglected. At regular intervals throughout the time that human beings have inhabited the earth we have been reminded of the total

The Natural Form of Man

knowledge we are capable of containing, and shown the form that is naturally ours, by men who have been directly inspired by Reality Itself to carry out this task.

These teachings have in part survived to this day in the form of the so-called "religions" and this explains the clear similarities that exist between them. But they are for the most part just archaeological fragments of original teachings which have been more or less distorted, vitiated, pieced together and adapted to man's lower nature. This has made them separate and antagonistic to each other, thus obscuring the fact that they are in reality successive manifestations of one continuously repeated teaching by men sent to other men by their Creator to show them and tell them how to be human.

Show and tell. The teaching has been both by example and by word. The two must go together for the necessary transformation to take place. In each case, a transmission took place from these Divinely inspired Messengers to the human communities where they appeared, whereby communities who had relapsed into ignorance and squalid sensual gratification, who had on a mass scale allowed their infantile self-form to take over and become the dominant influence in society, whereby these communities were purified, lifted up, and transformed by the transmissive process into radiant examples of true humanity.

They were communities where generosity, justice, compassion and humility were the rule rather than the exception and where people lived within clear moral limits which are in reality the picture of truly human nature. It is these Messengers from Reality together with their communities who gave rise to what are now known as the "world religions" but these have for the most part been altered beyond recognition, so that their original purpose, to show humans how to be human, has been all but completely obscured.

The one exception is the final complete version of the pure human teaching, the one revealed to Muhammad in Arabia in the early seventh century of the Christian era. It was transmitted by him to those around him and practised by them in Madina. It is known as Islam. This is where we must look if we desire to find the picture of the true human form and to know the knowledge that we are capable of containing, since, of all the teachings, it is the only one we know for certain to be completely intact. The message is there, unchanged by a single word, in the form of the Qur'an, giving us directly from Reality Itself the picture of the whole of existence and telling us exactly our part in it.

The example of the Messenger Muhammad ﷺ was minutely recorded showing us the perfection of the human form and how those around him took it on and therefore how we ourselves can do the same. This is not to say that some Muslims have not gone the way of previous communities and distorted and misapplied and misunderstood the original teaching. They clearly have. But the original teaching is still totally available and accessible for those who want it. The chain of transmission leading from the last of the Messengers, Muhammad, is unbroken and continues to this day.

An incident occurred during the life of the Prophet Muhammad ﷺ during which the component parts, which make up the whole human life transaction which is known as Islam, were comprehensively defined:

> 'Umar ibn al-Khattab said, "One day while we were sitting with the Messenger of Allah ﷺ there appeared before us a man whose clothes were exceedingly white and whose hair was exceedingly black. No trace of travel could be seen on him and none of us knew him. He walked up and sat down by the Prophet ﷺ. Resting his knees against his and placing the palms of his hands on his thighs, he said, 'O Muhammad! Tell me about Islam.' The Messenger of Allah ﷺ said, 'Islam is to testify that there is no god but Allah and that Muhammad is the Messenger of Allah, to establish the prayer, to pay the *zakat*, to fast Ramadan and to make the pilgrimage to the House if you are able to do so.' He said, 'You have spoken the truth,' and we were

amazed at him asking him and then saying that he had spoken the truth. He said, 'Then tell me about belief.' He said, 'It is to believe in Allah, His angels, His Books, His Messengers, and the Last Day, and to believe in the decree, both its good and its evil.' He said, 'You have spoken the truth.' He said, 'Then tell me about *ihsan*.' He said, 'It is to worship Allah as though you see Him for while you do not see Him, He sees you.' He said, 'Then tell me about the Hour.' He said, 'The one asked about it knows no more about it than the asker.' He said, 'Then tell me about its signs.' He said, 'That a slavegirl will give birth to her mistress and that you will see barefooted, destitute herdsmen competing in constructing lofty buildings.' Then he left but I stayed for a while. Then the Prophet ﷺ said, 'Umar, do you know who the questioner was?' I said, 'Allah and His Messenger know best.' He said, 'It was Jibril (Gabriel) who came to teach you your life-transaction.'" (Muslim)

This incident supplies the framework around which this book is constructed and ensures two things. All Muslims agree that this account provides an authentic designation of all the basic elements of Islam and so by including all of them all the basic beliefs and practices of Islam are covered. Secondly by limiting what is said to this framework the material discussed is necessarily restricted to only those things which are generally recognised to be fundamental to Islam and so shows many matters which often grab headlines to be the peripheral things they really are. Each of the elements mentioned is dealt with individually at some length and the result is a comprehensive overview of Islam which will hopefully dispel some commonly held misconceptions and give a clear picture of how the Muslims understand and practise their religion on a day to day basis.

ISLAM

is to testify that there is no god but Allah and that Muhammad is the Messenger of Allah, to establish the prayer, to pay the *zakat*, to fast Ramadan and to make the pilgrimage to the House if you are able to do so.

The Two *Shahadas*

to testify that there is no god but Allah ...
and that Muhammad is the Messenger of Allah

THE FIRST SHAHADA: THERE IS NO GOD BUT ALLAH

Various versions of this formula appear numerous times throughout the Qur'an and in many hadiths. A representative example from the Qur'an is:

Know then that there is no god but Allah
and ask forgiveness for your wrongdoing,
and for the men and women who believe.
Allah knows your activity and your repose. (47:20)

There is one creative power which is the source of all existence, from which everything that exists has poured forth and back to which everything is inevitably drawn when its lifespan comes to an end. This power sustains everything in existence and is totally aware of everything in existence at every moment. The material universe in which we live is merely an outer dimension of a multidimensional cosmic reality radiating out from that unitary source which includes other dimensions, the effects of which can be felt in this one. The human being is the potentially conscious locus of knowledge of this true nature of existence and there are very few people who, in their heart of hearts and their hours of greatest need, do not acknowledge the existence of God.

It says in the Qur'an that Allah only created men and jinn to worship Him and it is clear that worship in a general sense is a basic human instinct. Worship has demonstrably played a pivotal role in every society throughout the whole history of the human race. What the first *shahada* states unequivocally is that there can be no real object of worship except Allah. Over the ages human beings have turned many things into objects of worship: natural phenomena such as the sun and other heavenly bodies and mountains, oceans, trees and various animals on the surface of the earth, idols forged from metals or carved from stone, wood or clay, and in modern times more abstract things such as nationalism, communism, capitalism, scientific materialism and other ideologies of that kind, and also throughout time such mundane things as women, money and power.

These things represent open idolatry when people consciously worship them as gods but there is a more subtle way of turning things into objects of worship which happens when people invest things with attributes which properly speaking can only be ascribed to the Divine. One of the definitions the Qur'an gives of an object of worship is something which people turn to in the hope of gaining benefit or out of fear of receiving harm and it makes clear that nothing can, in real terms, be the cause of either benefit or harm for anyone except Allah alone. It is almost certain, however, that nearly all of us brought up and educated in this age of scientific materialism truly believe that harm and benefit come to us through many other things; all of us tend to attribute absolute effectiveness to the means through which we receive what comes to us. By doing this we in fact invest ordinary objects with intrinsic power and by doing this, because most of us now lack even an intellectual grasp of the theological truth, we imbue ordinary objects with attributes that can properly speaking only rightfully be ascribed to the Divine Reality. Even though we do it unconsciously, we are in fact turning all kinds of things into objects of worship. We are claiming that there are other gods besides Allah.

The Qur'an makes it abundantly clear, time and time again, that in reality nothing in existence has any real power except for Allah. This means that everything which happens in reality happens by Allah alone. We find *ayats* such as: *"It is He who sends down water from the sky from which We bring forth growth of every kind."* (6:99) Allah makes the rain fall; He makes the plants grow. *"Do they not see the birds suspended in mid-air up in the sky? Nothing holds them there except Allah."* (16:79) Flight is by Allah alone. *"It is He who created you from earth, then from a drop of sperm, then from a clot of blood, then He brings you out as infants."* (40:68) Allah is directly responsible for bringing us into the world. *"And when I am ill, it is He who heals me."* (26:80) Allah is the curer of illness.

The problem for us in this time is that all of us, from a very early age, have had precisely the opposite drilled into us. After Francis Bacon's famous dictum, "God works in nature only by secondary causes", theological truth and scientific truth parted company, and the depth to which the scientific materialist worldview has penetrated human consciousness cannot be overestimated. It is a thorough and continual indoctrination process with which we are bombarded every day of our lives. In the so-called "real world" the Divine has nothing to do with what goes on and we are told that, in fact, it is secondary causes that really make things happen.

According to this understanding, wind and rain are brought about by pressure changes in the atmosphere and the rain cycle; the cause of plant growth is the nitrogen cycle; flight occurs through the science of aerodynamics; our own birth is the result of the human conception and gestation process; illnesses are cured by the science of medicine. It is not that these various processes do not take place. They do. But they are not the reason for anything; they are not the cause of anything. According to the Qur'anic understanding there is no real connection between cause and effect. Effects coincide with causes but are not brought about by them. Both cause and effect are equally Divine creations. In every case both cause and effect are direct manifestations of Divine Power. The apparent cause has absolutely no inherent effectiveness.

This divorcing of cause from effect – implying as it does that it is not the food you eat that satisfies your hunger or the water you drink which quenches your thirst or the clothes you wear which keep you warm or the medicine you take which makes you better – seems to us in this time, at first sight, to make no sense at all. To say such a thing appears, in fact, to be nonsense. But this has not always been the case.

As long as theological truth rather than scientific truth formed the basis of the worldview of the majority of people, as it did right up to the end of the seventeenth century, then, although daily experience naturally led people to attribute effects to the causes which preceded them, there was at least an intellectual understanding that this connection was only an apparent one and that the direct manifestation of Divine Power is the real effective agent in the processes concerned. Indeed that continued to be the considered opinion of many extremely intelligent people in Europe up to the end of the eighteenth century. The empiricist philosopher George Berkeley, for instance, was extremely eloquent on the subject.

This discussion about the connection between cause and effect is vital in the context of understanding the first pillar of Islam because the statement that there is no god but Allah certainly entails the corollary that nothing happens without the direct involvement of Divine Will and Power and, therefore, clearly means that causes do not in reality bring about the effects which succeed them. The reason why it is almost impossible for anyone in this time to comprehend this in an authentic way really dates back to the scientific revolution of the seventeenth century which made people see the world they lived in a completely different way. Before then human beings had seen themselves as living at the centre of the universe with the sun and moon and stars revolving around them, above which were the celestial spheres of angelic activity all encompassed by the

Throne of God, whose unseen Hand moved and directed the whole affair.

After that time, however, because of the new understanding of the physical universe brought about by the invention of the telescope, people were forced to view themselves as the inhabitants of an insignificant mineral mass, a mere part of a minor planetary system, one of countless others lost in the unimaginable vastness of limitless space. The philosophical positions of such men as Descartes and Hobbes and the discoveries and theories of such men as Galileo and Newton posited a universe in which everything was now self-explanatory in terms of mutually dependent, internally self-consistent, interactive forces needing no extra-universal stimulus. There was no longer any need for God; everything was perfectly explicable without positing Divine intervention. The Divine had, to all intents and purposes, been expelled from the physical universe.

It is this materialist scientific view of existence that has now been drummed into virtually everyone in the world from earliest childhood. The scientific worldview has now intruded into every aspect of life and every corner of the earth and our education merely serves to reinforce it and articulate it and none of us has escaped its influence. Now almost everybody, educated or illiterate, rich or poor, Muslim or non-Muslim, views existence through a Galilean telescope and sees a Newtonian mechanistic universe with a mind permeated by Cartesian dualism and this has made it extremely difficult, if not impossible, for most people to be able to wholeheartedly accept that "There is no god but Allah" with all that it implies.

If this Newtonian view of existence had been shown to be a complete and exhaustive description of the way things really are, then it would indeed be difficult to see how the deep meaning of the first *shahada* could be relevant to it, but the truth is that, even within its own terms of reference, the Newtonian view has proved to be very incomplete and has been demonstrated to be an increasingly inadequate understanding of even the physical nature of existence.

The constituent parts of which matter is made up and the nature of the interaction between physical bodies has in fact turned out to be vastly more complex and mysterious than posited and envisaged by Galileo and Newton and their contemporaries and their eighteenth and nineteenth century successors.

As the twentieth century got under way ominous cracks started to appear in the previously unbreachable edifice of mechanistic science, not inflicted from outside – there was nothing left with the strength to do it – but from within. That very matter, the solid substance upon which the whole edifice rested and of which it was supposedly built, was suddenly discovered to be quite other than had been supposed. That very spirit of enquiry and experimentation that had been the energy behind the scientific revolution and had brought it into being was now to prove the undoing of many of its certainties.

Rutherford and Bohr showed conclusively that the atom, the supposedly basic building block of existence, was mostly composed of empty space. Max Planck showed that some of the basic premises of classical physics were clearly mistaken. Cracks were appearing throughout the proud edifice of classical physics and when Werner Heisenberg formulated his famous uncertainty principle, the cat was really among the pigeons. Rutherford's atomic model, with its minute particles coursing through empty space, had given a severe jolt to the classical concept of solid matter. Its transformation into a diffuse wave pattern had made things even worse. These worries, however, were completely eclipsed by Heisenberg's uncertainty relation, which put the very existence of solidity into question. Determinism, the singular connection of cause and effect, was rightly regarded as the rock on which natural philosophy was built and now with Heisenberg this safe basis, this basic premise, had been taken away.

This whole revolution in the understanding of the nature of matter is as important for our understanding of the nature of existence as were the discoveries of the seventeenth century. Rather than being the lifeless substance posited by Newton, mechanistically determined by being acted on by outside forces, matter turns out, at its very heart, to be composed of energy itself. Rather than being inert and predictable it is in fact highly dynamic and very mysterious. While the philosophical implications of all this have yet to make themselves generally felt in everyday life, they are certainly in evidence at the leading edge of every field of scientific enquiry. The atomic physicist Frithjof Capra expressed all this in a particularly lucid and eloquent way:

> When quantum mechanics – the theoretical foundation of atomic physics – was worked out in the 1920's, it became clear that even the sub-atomic particles were nothing like the solid objects of classical physics … At the sub-atomic level the solid material of classical physics dissolve into wave-like patterns of probabilities … A careful analysis of the process of observation in atomic physics has shown that the sub-atomic particles have no meaning as isolated entities but can only be understood as correlations between the preparation of an experiment and the subsequent measurement. This implies, however, that the Cartesian division between the I and the world cannot be made while dealing with atomic matter. Quantum mechanics thus reveals a basic oneness of the Universe. As we penetrate into matter, nature does not show us any isolated basic building blocks, but rather appears as a complicated web of relations between the various parts of the whole and these relations always include the observer in an essential way.

The point is that, as we have seen, the first *shahada*, the statement that there is no god but Allah, definitively implies that there is direct Divine participation in every physical process. The door to this participation was apparently slammed shut by the description of the universe posited by classical physics, a picture which has since been accepted as true by almost everyone on the planet. The new discoveries about the nature of matter, however, have completely changed that received picture and the door to understanding the reality of Divine participation in physical processes is once again open wide. So, whereas it has been very inaccessible for many people for many years, the statement, "there is no god but Allah", has once again become an authentic intellectual possibility for everyone. There is no valid reason why the first *shahada* should not be affirmed by every intelligent human being.

THE SECOND SHAHADA:
MUHAMMAD IS THE MESSENGER OF ALLAH

The times when the Prophet ﷺ is referred to in the Qur'an are extremely numerous but he is only mentioned by name on five occasions, one of which uses his other name: Ahmad.

> *And when 'Isa son of Maryam said,*
> *"Tribe of Israel, I am the Messenger of Allah to you,*
> *confirming the Torah which came before me*
> *and giving you the good news*
> *of a Messenger after me*
> *whose name is Ahmad." (61:6)*

> *But as for those who believe and do right actions*
> *and believe in what has been sent down*
> *to Muhammad –*
> *and it is the truth from their Lord –*
> *He will erase their bad actions from them*
> *and better their condition. (47:2)*

> *Muhammad is the Messenger of Allah,*
> *and those who are with him*
> *are fierce to the unbelievers,*
> *merciful to one another. (48:29)*

> *Muhammad is only a Messenger*
> *and he has been preceded by other Messengers.*
> *If he was to die or be killed,*

would you turn on your heels?
Those who turn on their heels
do not harm Allah in any way.
Allah will recompense the thankful. (3:144)

Muhammad is not the father of any of your men,
but the Messenger of Allah
and the Seal of the Prophets.
Allah has knowledge of everything. (33:40)

Human beings have always been given access to knowledge of the Divine through men who were by their nature open to it and were created to inform their fellow men about it. These chosen men told those around them about the Divine Unity and guided them to the way that they too could become aware of, and live in harmony with, this Reality. Some of these divinely inspired men received Divine Revelations, recorded in the form of written books, in which the truth of existence was made clear and by which human beings could be guided to a way of life in harmony with it. We still have access to this guidance in a complete form through the last of those naturally inspired by Reality Itself to guide people to It.

He was Muhammad ﷺ, the last of God's Messengers to the human race. Through him the Qur'an, the final Divine revelation containing complete guidance for all human needs until the end of time, was revealed. In his life he demonstrated what it is to be a completely fulfilled human being, embodying every perfection of character, and showing us how someone totally submitted to the Divine conducts their day-to-day affairs in the face of all the contingencies of the ordinary human situation.

HIS LIFE

He was the son of 'Abdullah, son of 'Abdul-Muttalib, son of Hashim of the tribe of Quraysh, descendant of Isma'il (Ishmael), son of Ibrahim (Abraham), and was born in Makka in about 570 CE. His father died before his birth and his mother Amina died while he was still a young boy, but he found a protector and a guardian first in his grandfather 'Abdu'l-Muttalib, and then, on his death, in his uncle Abu Talib. His childhood was very simple. He was sent, as was the custom with good Makkan families, to a wet nurse named Halima in a desert tribe. He received no formal education of any kind and, as a boy, would look after his family's herd of sheep and goats in the hills surrounding Makka.

On one occasion he accompanied his uncle on a caravan to Syria and on this journey met a Christian hermit called Bahira who told his uncle that his young nephew would be the prophet of his people. When he was twenty-five years old, he again made the same journey, this time as a trader in the service of a wealthy widow named Khadija. As a result of his success and from hearing reports of the excellence of his character, Khadija married her young agent. They lived together for twenty-six years and she was the mother of his children and stood by him during the difficult years when he was trying to spread Islam among the people of Makka.

It was his custom every year to spend the month of Ramadan alone in a cave on a mountain near Makka. In his fortieth year, nearly at the end of this month, he heard during the night a voice which said to him: "Read!" He replied: "I cannot read." Again the voice came: "Read!" Again he replied, awestruck: "I cannot read." For the third time, the voice commanded: "Read!" He said, "What should I read?" The voice said: *"Read in the Name of your Lord who created. He created man from a clot...."* (96:1-2; Sira Ibn Hisham) This was the beginning of the revelation of the Qur'an, which continued, intermittently, until just before his death, twenty-three years later. The voice told him that he was the Messenger of Allah and raising his eyes he saw the angel Jibril who was the means by which the revelation was conveyed to him from the Creator of the universe.

His first thought was that he had gone mad, but he was reassured by his wife Khadija and gradually, as the revelation continued, his reluctance left him and he accepted the awesome task of being the Messenger of the Lord of creation. During the first three

The Natural Form of Man

years after this event, he told only his immediate circle about what had happened. His wife Khadija, his adopted son 'Ali, his freed slave Zayd, and his friend Abu Bakr were among the first to accept what he said and to agree to follow him.

Then he received the command to "arise and warn" and he began to talk openly to the people of Makka. He pointed out to them the stupidity of idol worship in the face of the clear proofs of the Divine Unity manifest in the creation. He gave them the good news of the delights of the Garden in the Next World for those who believe in the One God and act upon their belief and warned them of the torments of the Fire for those who reject that belief. Seeing their way of life threatened by this teaching, the clans of Quraysh became hostile and started to persecute his followers and to insult him.

In spite of this, the number of Muslim steadily increased and so Quraysh tried to stop him with bribes, even offering to make him their king if he would only compromise with them and stop attacking their false gods. By his words and example, he was undermining and endangering the structure of their society and the basis of their wealth. The savage persecution of his followers which followed led the Prophet ﷺ to send a group of them to Abyssinia where they found temporary asylum under the Christian king there. However, Islam was further strengthened when 'Umar ibn al-Khattab accepted the Prophet ﷺ. He was one of the strongest and most respected of Quraysh and until this time had been one of the staunchest opponents of Islam.

In their frustration and rage, Quraysh confined the whole of the Prophet's clan to a ravine for three years forbidding all dealings with them. During this time, his wife Khadija and his uncle and protector Abu Talib died and an attempt that he made to take Islam to the nearby city of Ta'if met with failure and rejection. It was at this seemingly low ebb that his famous *Isra* or Night Journey took place, during which Muhammad went from Makka to Jerusalem, and then he was taken up through the seven heavens, on the *Mi'raj* or Ascension, where he was brought face to face with the Divine Presence and shown the true nature of his own being and the honour in which he was held by his Lord, the Divine Reality.

Shortly after this, a small group of men from a city named Yathrib, some distance north of Makka, listened to him when they came to Makka for the pilgrimage. They accepted him as Prophet 🐝 and returned to their city with a Muslim teacher. The following year they returned with seventy-three new Muslims and invited the Prophet 🐝 to come to live in their city as their leader. From then on the Muslims began to leave Makka and to settle in Yathrib and finally the Prophet 🐝, evading an attempt to murder him, escaped from the city of his birth and travelled with Abu Bakr to Yathrib, which became renamed as *al-Madina al-Munawwara*, the Enlightened City. This event is known as the Hijra and marks the beginning of the Muslim calendar and of the Muslim community as a political reality.

Soon after settling in Madina the Prophet 🐝 was ordered by his Lord to fight his enemies, although up to this time there had been no attempt at self-defence. The first expeditions were very small and there was almost no fighting in them. In the second year after the Hijra, Quraysh sent an army of a thousand men, ostensibly to protect a caravan from Syria. The Prophet 🐝 had assembled an army of just over three hundred men who, because they had not come out anticipating serious battle, were completely ill-equipped in terms of weapons, armour and mounts. The two sides met at a place called Badr. The Muslims led by the Prophet 🐝, with complete trust in Allah in their hearts and reinforcement from the angelic world, won a total victory and killed many of the leaders of Quraysh. The enmity of Quraysh increased but Islam was, from this time on, firmly established in the land.

The following year, Quraysh marched against Madina and the Muslims met them at the mountain of Uhud, a short distance from the city. Despite a serious numerical disadvantage, the Muslims would have won a victory except that greed for the spoils

The Natural Form of Man

led a band of archers to leave their position and the Muslims were defeated. This defeat subsequently led to the murder of Muslims who travelled to spread Islam and to open hostility from the Jewish inhabitants of Madina, encouraged by disaffected elements within the Muslim community.

In the fifth year of the Hijra, Quraysh formed a coalition with some other tribes and again attacked Madina, this time coming with about ten thousand men. The Prophet ﷺ had organised the digging of a deep ditch as a defence for the city and the affair became known as the Battle of the Ditch. A tribe of Jews from Madina, who had previously agreed a treaty of mutual support and protection with the Muslims, joined the Makkans. However, confused by the ditch and discouraged by the suspicion of their Jewish allies and a bitter wind which blew for three days and nights, they packed up and left without offering battle. The Jewish tribe were severely punished for their treacherous behaviour, the judgement on them passed by an ally whom they themselves had nominated, his sentence taken from the Torah itself.

In the same year, the Prophet ﷺ decided to take a company of fourteen hundred men to Makka to perform *Hajj*. They camped at a place called al-Hudaybiyya just outside the city, but were prevented from entering. Envoys were sent by Quraysh, and the Prophet ﷺ made a treaty which appeared to be disadvantageous to the Muslims and they returned to Madina without setting foot in the Holy City. However, this treaty, which stopped the fighting between Quraysh and the Muslims, proved in fact a great victory and Islam spread with greater speed than ever before. Under the terms of the treaty, Quraysh had agreed to evacuate Makka the following year for three days while the Muslims visited the city and performed *'Umra*. This was to be the first time that the Prophet ﷺ and his Companions had visited Makka for seven years.

In the following year, the Prophet ﷺ sent an army of three thousand to face an attack from the Byzantine Emperor in Syria. They attacked fearlessly a hundred thousand men, fighting until three leaders had been killed. The few who remained retired and returned to Madina. Then a tribe in alliance with Quraysh broke the treaty they had made at al-Hudaybiyya and the Prophet ﷺ marched with ten thousand men against Quraysh in Makka. They conquered the city without any bloodshed and the Prophet ﷺ proclaimed a general amnesty. He freely forgave the people who had unceasingly persecuted him since the beginning of Islam. They became Muslims and the only destruction was of the idols around the Ka'ba. The Prophet ﷺ set about subduing the remaining hostile tribes, winning a victory at Hunayn, and he besieged and won over the city of Ta'if whose people had rejected him ten years earlier.

In the ninth year of the Hijra, the Muslims of Madina were tested by Allah. The Prophet ﷺ called for all the Muslims to go with him at the hottest time of the year on a gruelling expedition to a place far to the north called Tabuk to counter a force of the Byzantine Romans. Some went and some stayed behind. The expedition returned without fighting. The same year was known as the Year of Deputations and people came from all parts of Arabia to enter Islam and swear allegiance to the Prophet ﷺ.

In the tenth year of the Hijra, the Prophet ﷺ led the Farewell *Hajj* at which there were one hundred and forty thousand Muslims. In an address on Mount Arafat, he reminded them of the duties of Islam and that they would be called to account for their actions, and then he asked them if he had truly delivered the guidance he had been sent with. The reply was: "By Allah, yes!" and he said, "O Allah, You are witness." Soon after his return to Madina, he became ill and died with his head in the lap of his most loved wife, 'A'isha.

During the last ten years of his life, he led twenty-seven campaigns in nine of which there was fierce fighting. He planned and sent out thirty more. He personally supervised every detail of administration and himself judged every case, being accessible to every suppliant. He destroyed idol worship and replaced the arrogance and violence, drunkenness and immorality of the Arabs, by humility and compassion, harmony and generosity, creating a truly illuminated society. By the time he died, he had fulfilled his Divinely appointed task by establishing, under Divine guidance, a flourishing human community with a just political, economic and legal structure which protected a radiant, compassionate social reality and permitted the flowering of as deep a spirituality as has ever been witnessed on the earth's surface.

His Character

In an environment accustomed to arrogant violence he was mild-tempered and beautifully mannered. He was never insulting and never looked down on illness or poverty. He honoured nobility and rewarded according to worth, giving each person what was most fitting to their needs. He never paid homage to wealth and power, but called all those who came to him to the worship of Allah.

He would always be the first to greet whomever he met and would never be the first to withdraw his hand. He was endlessly patient with all who came to him for advice or help, not minding the ignorance of the uneducated nor the coarseness of the ill-bred. On one occasion, a Bedouin came to him asking for something and tugged so violently at his clothes that he ripped a piece right off. Muhammad ﷺ laughed and gave the man what he wanted.

It was one of his qualities that he had time for all who needed him. He showed regard for his visitors to the point of giving up his own place or spreading his cloak for them to sit on; and if they refused, he would urge them until they accepted. He gave all his guests his complete attention so that all without exception felt that they were the most honoured.

Of all men, he was the least prone to anger and the most ready to be pleased. The mistakes of his Companions were not mentioned and he never blamed or reviled anyone. His servant Anas was with him for ten years and not once in all that time did Muhammad ﷺ take him to task even by so much as asking why he had not done something. He loved to hear good things about his Companions and regretted their absence. He visited the sick even in the parts of Madina that were furthest from his house and the most difficult to get to. He attended feasts and accepted the invitations of slaves and free men alike. He accompanied funeral processions and prayed over the graves of his companions. Wherever he went he walked unguarded, even among people who were known to be unfriendly to him.

He had a powerful melodious voice and, although he was silent for long periods at a time, he would always speak when the occasion demanded. When he spoke, he was extraordinarily eloquent and precise, and his sentences were beautifully constructed and so cohesive that those who heard them – whoever they were – could easily understand and remember his words. He would speak sweetly and playfully when he was with his wives; and with his companions he was the most smiling and laughing of men, admiring what they said and joining in with them. He was never angry for his own sake, or for any matter connected with this world, but when he became angry for the sake of Allah, nothing whatever could stand in his way. When he directed someone to a place, he would point with his whole hand. When he was pleased with something, he turned his palms up. When he was speaking, he placed his palms together. When he talked to someone, he would turn towards them with his whole body. Whatever he did, he would do it to the full.

His generosity was such that whenever he was asked for anything he was never known to say no. He once went on giving sheep to a Bedouin who kept asking for more until they filled a valley between two mountains and the man was overwhelmed. He would never go to bed until all the money in his house had been distributed to the poor and he would frequently give away from his year's store of grain, so that he and his family would be without before the year was up. He used to ask people about their needs without them coming to him and would give them what they wanted. As he was generous with his few possessions, so he was generous with himself, giving unceasingly, advice, help, kindness, and forgiveness, and overflowing love.

He loved poverty and was continually to be found with the poor. His life was as simple as possible. He always sat on the ground, and often when he was with his Companions he would sit in the last row so that visitors could not distinguish him among them. He ate from a dish on a cloth on the ground and never used a table. He slept on the ground on a mat of palm fibre, the marks of which showed on his skin, though he did not refuse more comfort if it was offered to him.

He and his family would frequently go hungry and there were months at a stretch when no smoke would rise from his or his wives' houses because they had only dates and water and no food to cook or oil for the lamps. But on other occasions, when food was available, he ate well. He said that the best meal was the one with the most hands eating it. He never criticised food. If he liked it, he ate it, and if he didn't, he left it.

He used to tie up the male camel and feed the animals used for carrying water. He swept his room, soled his shoes, patched his clothes, milked the ewe, ate with his slaves whom he dressed as he dressed himself, and carried what he bought from the market place to his house. He said, "O Allah, make me live and die and be raised up with poor," (Ibn Majah, al-Hakim, at-Tirmidhi, at-Tabarani) and at his death, he left no money at all.

He would wear whatever was at hand, provided it was lawful, though he particularly liked green and white garments. When he wore a new garment, he would give an old one away. Sometimes he would wear coarse wool. He had a striped cloak from the Yemen of which he was particularly fond. He loved perfumes and would buy the best that were available. The only possessions of which he was particularly fond and of which he took great care were his swords, his bow and his armour, which he used fearlessly in the many expeditions he led.

Above all, it was through him that the Qur'an was revealed and his whole life was a continual manifestation of its teachings.

He was the perfect example to his community, both of how they should be in regard to each other and the world, and also of how they should be with their Lord, the Creator of the Universe. He showed them how to purify themselves and how and when to prostrate before Allah. He showed them how and when to fast. He showed them how and when to give. He showed them how to fight in the Way of Allah. He led them in prayer and prostrated alone during the night until his feet became swollen. When he was asked why, he said, "Should I not be a thankful slave?" (Abu Dawud) He had a prayer for every action and he would never rise nor sit without mentioning Allah. All his actions were performed with the intention of pleasing his Lord. He taught his community everything that would bring them closer to Allah and warned them against everything that would distance them from Allah.

He inspired love and awe in all who met him and his Companions loved and revered him more than their families, their possessions, and more even than themselves. His close companion and friend Abu Bakr as-Siddiq, rather than disturb his beloved Prophet ﷺ who was asleep at the time, once put his foot in a hole where there was a snake, which bit him. His son-in-law and nephew 'Ali risked being murdered in his place, and there are many more accounts of the devotion he inspired among those who followed him.

His Lord said of him in the Qur'an: *"Indeed you are truly vast in character"* (68:4), and he himself said, "I was only sent to perfect good character." (Al-Bukhari, Muslim) The unanimity of reaction of those closest to him and the description of him which has come down to us from them show a man of such perfection of character that there can remain no doubt about the truth of the message and guidance which he brought – the Way of Islam.

Salat/Prayer

to establish the prayer...

There are references to the prayer everywhere in the Qur'an. There is scarcely a page that does not mention it in one way or another. Here are a few, which are representative of many many others:

Establish the prayer at each end of the day
  and in the first part of the night.
Good actions eradicate bad actions.
This is a reminder for people who pay heed. (11:114)

When you are safe again do the prayer in the normal way.
  The prayer is prescribed for the believers at specific times.
                                                    (4:103)

Recite what has been revealed to you of the Book
  and establish the prayer.
The prayer precludes indecency and wrongdoing.
  And remembrance of Allah is greater still.
    Allah knows what you do. (29:45)

Seek help in steadfastness and prayer.
But that is a very hard thing, except for the humble:
  those who are aware that they will meet their Lord
  and that they will return to Him. (2:44-45)

PURIFICATION

O you who believe!
When you get up to do the prayer,
  wash your faces and your hands
  and your arms to the elbows,
  and wipe over your heads,
  and your feet to the ankles.
If you are in a state of major impurity,
  then purify yourselves completely. (5:7)

In order to perform the prayer it is first necessary to purify yourself with water. There are two acts of purification, a major one – *ghusl* – which involves washing the whole body and a minor one – *wudu* – in which only certain parts of the body are involved. Prior to any act of purification there is the very necessary cleansing of oneself after going to the lavatory.

Ghusl is necessary in order to enter Islam, and after sexual intercourse and sexual discharge and, in the case of women, at the end of menstrual periods and the end of the period of bleeding which follows childbirth. It comprises first of all washing the hands and the private parts, then performing a complete *wudu* washing each limb once only. When washing the hair you first wet the fingers of both hands and then comb them through the hair of your head and beard, following that by pouring three cupped handfuls of water over your hair. After that you complete it by washing all the rest of the body.

Wudu, which is nullified by going to the lavatory, breaking wind, and sleeping, is necessary for every prayer. It is good to begin *wudu*, and indeed all other actions, by saying *bismillah* – "In the name of Allah". You need a supply of pure water sufficient to enable you to complete the act of purification and you start by washing your hands three times with the water. Then, taking water in your cupped right hand, you rinse out your mouth three times, during which it is good to rub the outside of your teeth with the index finger and thumb of your right hand. Taking water in your cupped right hand once more, you sniff a little up into your nose and blow it out again holding your nose lightly between the thumb and index finger of your left hand. You do this three times.

Then you take water with both hands and, starting from your hairline at the top of your forehead, let the water run down your face and wash your face all over from the top to the end of the chin and from ear to ear. If you have a beard, wipe over it unless it is very sparse in which case you should make sure that water penetrates to the skin. This should be done three times. This is also the time to affirm your intention so that what you are doing truly becomes an act of purification enabling you to stand before your Lord in prayer and not merely a splashing of water over various parts of your body.

Then you take some more water with your right hand and let it run down your right arm to the elbow, while at the same time using your left hand to rub the outside and inside of the right arm up to and including the elbow, as well as the whole of the right hand, making sure that water goes between the fingers of the right hand by running the fingers of the left hand through them. You do this three times and then, after transferring some water to the left hand from the right, you wash the left arm and hand in the same way three times, rubbing it with the right hand.

The next thing is wiping over the head. To do this, you pour some water from the right hand into the left and then shake off any excess, leaving both hands wet. You place your thumbs on your temples and put the tips of your fingers together so that your hands cover the hairline at the top of your forehead and then wipe right over your head from the hairline to the nape of the neck, making sure the entire head is covered. Then you bring your hands forward to the front again so that they end up where they started. Wetting your hands in the same way once more, you wipe the inside and outside of your ears, using the thumb and index finger of both hands.

The last act of *wudu* is washing the feet. Starting with the right foot, you scoop water onto it with the right hand and rub it with the left, making sure that water covers every part of it, including the ankle and the heel and between the toes. You do this three times. Then you wash the left foot in the same way three times, again scooping water onto it with the right hand and rubbing it with the left. This completes the act of purification known as *wudu*.

It is good to seal *wudu* by repeating the *shahada* immediately after finishing it, because the Messenger of Allah ﷺ said: "Whoever does *wudu*, and does it well, and then raises his sight heavenwards and says, 'I witness that there is no god but Allah, alone and without partner, and I witness that Muhammad is His slave and Messenger,' the eight gates of the Garden are opened for him and he may enter by whichever one he chooses." (An-Nasa'i, Ibn Majah, al-Hakim)

In the event that no water is available or that using it would be damaging to the health, Muslims are permitted to purify themselves with bare earth or rock, by striking lightly on the dry earth or rock with both hands, then shaking off any surplus dust, wiping over the face, then repeating the striking and wiping hands and arms. This is called *tayammum*.

Once you have purified yourself in this way you are ready to perform the ritual prayer of Islam which is known as the *salat*. The *salat* is made up of a series of regular specified movements that repeat themselves in cycles known as *rak'ats*. In each *rak'at* there is a period of standing upright, followed by bowing, followed by a return to the upright position, followed by two prostrations with a short period of sitting between them. The *salat* is obligatory five times every day for every Muslim and the number of *rak'ats* varies according to the particular time of day involved.

PRAYER TIMES

The first time is from dawn – which is when light first becomes visible along the eastern horizon – until shortly before sunrise. The prayer at this time is called *Salat as-Subh* (or *Fajr*, the Dawn Prayer) and is made up of two *rak'ats*. The second time of prayer is from just after the sun reaches the zenith at midday until midway through the afternoon. This prayer is known as *Salat adh-Dhuhr* (the Midday Prayer) and consists of four *rak'ats*. The third time starts midway through the afternoon and ends an hour or so before sunset. This prayer is called *Salat al-'Asr* (the Afternoon Prayer) and also contains four *rak'ats*. The fourth time is the briefest, lasting only from immediately after sunset until approximately fifteen minutes have elapsed. This prayer is *Salat al-Maghrib* (the Sunset Prayer) and consists of three *rak'ats*. The final and fifth time of prayer is from when all the redness of the sunset has left the sky until a third of the night has passed. The name of this prayer is *Salat al-'Isha* (the Night Prayer) and has four *rak'ats*.

One other obligatory group prayer that should be mentioned is *Salat al-Jumu'a* – the Prayer of Gathering – which takes the place of the midday prayer every Friday and which all the men of any Muslim community must attend in the particular mosques where it is held. Women may also attend but it is not obligatory for them.

These are the obligatory times when every Muslim must do the *salat*, and when it is best done by the men as a group in a mosque, but there are many other occasions when the *salat* can be and indeed is done individually on a voluntary basis by nearly all Muslims. There are also special prayers held during the early morning of the two great feast days of Islam, the *Eid al-Fitr*, which marks the end of the month of Ramadan, and the *Eid al-Adha*, which takes place annually during the *Hajj*. These, which are properly held outside in the open on a large enough space of ground to encompass people from a number of mosques rather than inside mosques, are each known as *Salat al-Eid* (the feast prayer) and it is recommended for everyone in the community to attend, including women and children.

DOING THE PRAYER

To perform the *salat* it is necessary to be wearing reasonably loose opaque clothing which covers the body properly – for men that means from the neck to below the knee and for women the whole body except the face and hands; it is also essential that your body and clothing and the place where you are praying are free from any impurities; and you must also be facing in the direction of the *qibla*, which is towards the Sacred Mosque in Makka.

After making a clear inward intention for the particular prayer you are proposing to perform, you stand facing the *qibla* with your head level, your eyes lowered and your feet slightly apart. When praying with others in the mosque you stand shoulder to shoulder without leaving any gaps in the row. You raise both hands with the palms facing forwards and downwards, and then you lower them to your sides while saying *"Allahu akbar"* (Allah is greater). This is known as the *takbir al-ihram* and marks the beginning of the prayer, from which point nothing other than the *salat* is permissible until the end of it. Then you recite *Surat al-Fatiha* (the opening *sura* of the Qur'an) followed by another *sura* or passage from the Qur'an. This recitation must be done in Arabic and is either silent or out loud depending on the prayer being performed.

THE FATIHA:

1   *Al-hamdu lillahi rabbi'l-'alameen*
2   *Ar-Rahmani'r-Raheem*
3   *Maliki yawmi'd-deen*
4   *Iyyaka na'budu*
        wa iyyaka nasta'een

5   *Ihdina's-sirata'l-mustaqeem*
6   *sirata'lladheena an'amta 'alayhim*
7   *ghayri'l-maghdoubi 'alayhim*
          wa la'd-dalleen.

After it one says silently *Ameen*. The translation of the *Fatiha* is as follows:

The Natural Form of Man

1   *Praise be to Allah, the Lord of all the worlds,*
2   *the All-Merciful, the Most Merciful,*
3   *the King of the Day of Judgment.*
4   *You alone we worship.*
          You alone we ask for help.

5   *Guide us on the Straight Path,*
6   *the Path of those whom You have blessed,*
7   *not of those with anger on them,*
          nor of the misguided.

When you have finished reciting you say *"Allahu akbar"* and bend forward from the waist until your back is parallel to the ground, placing your hands on your knees. This bowing position is called *ruku'* and you remain in it for several seconds glorifying Allah. Then saying the words *"sami'a'llahu liman hamidah"* (Allah hears those who praise Him), you stand up again and, after remaining upright for a few moments, you say *"Allahu akbar"* and, bending your knees and putting your hands palms downwards on the ground in front of you, you go into the position of prostration known as *sujud*. In this position your forehead, nose, palms, knees and feet should be touching the ground. Your palms should be parallel with your head, with the fingers facing forwards, and your elbows should be raised off the ground. Your feet should be upright with the toes bent facing forwards.

You remain in this position for several seconds or at least until still, glorifying Allah and making supplication to Him, and then, saying *"Allahu akbar"*, you sit back into the kneeling/ sitting position known as *julus*. You either sit on your left foot, which is folded under you, or on your left buttock with your left foot under your right leg whose foot remains upright and you place your hands palm down over your knees. After a second or two, during which you ask Allah for forgiveness, you say *"Allahu akbar"* once more and return to *sujud* where you again remain for several seconds glorifying Allah and making supplication to

Him. With this second prostration you complete your first *rak'at*. Then, pushing yourself off the ground with your hands, you stand upright again saying *"Allahu akbar"* as you stand.

Once you are still, you recite the *Fatiha* as you did in the first *rak'at* followed by a different *sura* or passage from the Qur'an and you follow exactly the same sequence as before, only this time, instead of standing up after the second prostration, you sit back again in the *julus* position a second time. Then you recite the formula known as the *tashahhud* (witnessing).

Frequently your *salat* will finish after two *rak'ats* and when that is the case you continue reciting after the *tashahhud*, adding the formula asking for blessings on the Prophet Muhammad 鑶 and his ancestor the Prophet Ibrahim. Then you end your prayer by turning your head to the right and saying the words *"as-salamu 'alaykum"* (peace be upon you) as you do so.

If, however, the prayer is one of more than two *rak'ats*, after completing the *tashahhud*, you stand up again and, once you are upright, say *"Allahu akbar"* and then you recite the *Fatiha* on its own. When you have done that you continue the sequence as in the other *rak'ats*. If you are praying *Salat al-Maghrib* (Sunset Prayer), which is three *rak'ats* in length, you sit back after your second *sujud* of the third *rak'at* as you did in the second *rak'at* and you do the *tashahhud* and the prayer of asking blessings on the Prophet 鑶 as already described and you finish your *salat* with the *salam*. But if the *salat* is one of four *rak'ats*, you stand up again after the second *sujud* of this third *rak'at* and do another *rak'at*, reciting the *Fatiha* alone and you complete your prayer, in the way already described, at the end of the fourth *rak'at*.

GENERAL REMARKS ABOUT THE PRAYER

To understand something of the importance of the *salat* it is only necessary to look at the way it was prescribed for mankind. It was what the Prophet 鑶 brought back from his Lord when he was taken up through the seven heavens on his Ascension and then went on into the very presence of Allah. We know

The Natural Form of Man

that on that occasion he was given fifty daily prayers, which were gradually reduced to the five that are now performed – five which by the generosity of Allah receive the reward of the original fifty. This means that the *salat* embodies the secret of the absolute pinnacle of all possible human experience, the face to face meeting of the Prophet ﷺ with Allah, blessed is He and exalted.

Many Muslims do not realise that the words of the *tashahhud*, which are recited in the sitting position of the prayer are a record of the exchange which took place between the Prophet ﷺ and his Lord, may He be exalted, during that awesome encounter. The Prophet ﷺ said: *"at-tahiyyatu lillah az-zakiyatu lillah at-tayyibatu's-salawatu lillah"* (All greetings are for Allah and all purity belongs to Allah and all good prayers belong to Allah); then Allah said: *"as-salamu 'alayka ayyuha'n-nabiyyu wa rahmatullahi wa barakatuh"* (Peace be upon you O Prophet and the mercy of Allah and his blessing); to which the Prophet ﷺ responded: *"as-salamu 'alayna wa 'ala 'ibadillahi's-salihin"* (Peace be upon us and upon all the right-acting slaves of Allah). Each time Muslims do the prayer, therefore, they are in a way reconnecting with that supreme human possibility and opening themselves to the highest potential of their own individual consciousness.

The *salat* is the greatest of the means that Allah, the Exalted, has given mankind to ensure that they remain on the path of Truth, the path which leads to His mercy and forgiveness and to every good thing in both the worlds. It is quite literally a lifeline, that which connects people to the Living Who never dies, and the fact that Allah has made it obligatory five times every day guarantees that that connection will not be severed. The Prophet ﷺ likened *salat* to a river in which someone bathes five times every day and asked those with him whether any dirt would remain on their body after that? The Companions present answered that of course none would. (Al-Bukhari, Muslim, at-Tirmidhi, an-Nasa'i)

So the regular performance of *salat* prevents the connection between each person and their Lord from becoming clogged up. It wipes out all minor wrong actions committed between them. *Salat* is the greatest of the pillars of Islam after the two *shahadas*. Allah has made it obligatory so that people's ranks may be elevated by it, their good actions multiplied, their wrong actions, mistakes and evil deeds fall from them, and by it He admits them to the Gardens of Paradise and saves them from the Fire of Hell.

However, like every blessing, *salat* is a double-edged sword. For those who safeguard it, it will prove to be a source of light in the heart, in the grave and on the Day of Rising. It will provide them with the evidence and proof they need to save them from painful punishment on that Day because as we know from Yahya ibn Sa'id in the *Muwatta*: "The first of the actions of a person to be considered on the Day of Rising is their *salat*. If it is accepted from them, the rest of their actions are considered; if not, then none of the rest of their actions will be considered." But if people neglect it or devalue it, it will correspondingly count against them on the Day when they need it most. Allah, may He be blessed and exalted, says in *Sura Maryam* (Mary):

> *An evil generation succeeded them*
> *who neglected the salat*
> *and followed their appetites.*
> *They will plunge into the Valley of Evil. (19:59)*

And the Prophet 🕮 said:

> Between a man and association of partners with Allah
> and unbelief there is abandonment of the prayer. (Muslim)

The position the prayer holds in Islam is comparable to the main pole in a tent – if it is there the tent can be used and all the other poles, guy ropes and pegs will find their place; if it is not there then the whole structure collapses and is useless. In this context it is important to remember that Allah, exalted is He, does not merely command people to do *salat* but rather instructs them to establish it, which, as all the Qur'anic commentators are agreed, implies much more than simply performing the necessary number of *rak'ats* at a given time. First, it includes all the preconditions of purity, place, dress, and direction mentioned earlier but also certain social and political dimensions that are integral to the performance of *salat*.

These are most evident at *Salat al-Jumu'a* every Friday when it is an obligation for all the men of the community to attend the prayer. Indeed, it could be said that the political dimensions of a given community are defined by the attendance at its *Jumu'a* prayer. It is, however, clear that the early Muslims considered the men doing the prayer together in the mosque at all times an essential part of establishing *salat*.

There is a well-known hadith of the Prophet ﷺ which makes it clear that for men *salat* in a group is twenty-seven times better than *salat* alone. (Sa'id ibn Mansur) It is clear that the original understanding of this statement took it as referring to the communal prayer done in the mosque behind the imam of the community. Women are not required to pray in the mosque although it is acceptable for them to do so. This importance for men of the *salat* behind the imam of the mosque is the reason why Imam Malik, following the practice of the first right-acting generations in Madina, and Imam Abu Hanifa both forbade people to form another group prayer in the mosque after the one performed behind the imam for a particular prayer time had been done.

Imam Malik said that Islam would only later be right by what made it right to start with and there can be no doubt that establishing *salat* in the way it was established by the first community is the essential first step to establishing Islam. Without the main pole being erected it is wishful thinking to suppose that the rest of the structure of Islam can be put into place.

The position of the first community on this matter is made

very clear to us by the uncompromising words of the great Companion, 'Abdullah ibn Mas'ud, who said:

> Whoever desires to meet Allah as a Muslim tomorrow should safeguard these five prayers when the call for them is given. Allah prescribed for His Prophet ﷺ all the norms of guidance, and the establishment of the prayer is one of them. If you do the prayer in your houses, as someone who fails to come to the prayer in the mosque does, you have abandoned the *Sunna* of your Prophet ﷺ. If you abandon the *Sunna* of your Prophet, you will never be guided. You have seen us and not one of us failed to come to *salat* in the mosque other than hypocrites whose hypocrisy was known, or people who were ill. People used to come to the prayer supported between two men until they were stood upright in the row. (Muslim)

More evidence of the further ramifications of the *salat* and how it extends into the social sphere can be found in various hadiths of the Prophet ﷺ.

> Al-Bara' ibn 'Azib said: "The Messenger of Allah ﷺ used to go between the rows from one end to the other, pushing our chests and shoulders. He would say, 'Do not be disunited or your hearts will become disunited.' He used to say, 'Allah and His angels bless the first row.'" (Ahmad ibn Hanbal, Abu Dawud, an-Nasa'i)

> Ibn 'Umar reported that the Messenger of Allah ﷺ said, "Make the rows straight, stand shoulder to shoulder and close up the gaps. Give way to your brothers and do not leave any openings for Shaytan. Allah will connect with anyone who connects up the row and Allah will break off from anyone who makes a break in a row." (Ahmad, Abu Dawud, at-Tabarani, al-Bayhaqi)

These hadiths and a number of similar ones not only tell us how we should behave in the *salat* – although they certainly do that – but also clearly indicate that the way people perform the *salat* is a kind of benchmark for their lives, both as individuals and as a community. The *salat* is a reflection in miniature of people's lives as a whole. As we pray so we live. This is, in fact, a vital aspect of the *salat* for those who do it, because if you really reflect honestly on the way you pray, you can learn a great deal about yourself. Do you do it on time and if not why not? How is your physical comportment in it; are you too rigid or too floppy? What is your level of concentration in it and what tends to distract you most during it?

These and many other points, which might be elaborated on, tell you a lot about your life as a whole. And more than simply giving you insight into your own state and, indeed, that of the whole community, it also gives you the chance of doing something about things that are not as they should be. It works the other way round as well. If you correct any defects or imbalances you have noticed at the microcosmic level of the prayer, not superficially but by going to the source of the problem and addressing it, you will inevitably find that at the macrocosmic level of your daily life that same defect or imbalance which manifested itself in the *salat* will fade away there as well. This is yet another benefit among innumerable others which can be derived from this incalculably precious gift Allah has given to the human race.

There is no end to the things that might be said about the *salat*, and many lengthy books have been devoted to it, but it would be useful to add to this brief general look at it a few things great scholars of the past have had to say about it.

Shaykh Ibn Ata'illah al-Iskandari, may Allah have mercy on him, says in his *Hikam*:

> Since Allah knows that you easily become bored,
>> He has varied acts of obedience for you.
> Since He knows that you are prone to over-eagerness,
>> He has forbidden you to do them at certain times.
> This is so that your aspiration will be for the

establishment of the prayer,
not just for the prayer itself.
Not everyone who does the prayer establishes it.

He knows you are weak,
so He has made the prayers few in number.
He knows that you have need of His
overflowing favour
so He has multiplied His blessings to you in them.

Prayer is purification for the hearts,
a means of opening onto the unseen worlds.
Prayer is the place of intimate conversation,
a mine of mirrored purity.
The fields of the secrets stretch out into the
vastness within it.
Lights rise in it and beam out their radiance.

Shaykh Moulay al-'Arabi ad-Darqawi, may Allah have mercy on him, says in one of his letters:

Whoever desires to save himself, to make himself happy, to have his faults veiled, to gain the pleasure of his Lord, to have his inner eye opened, to have gifts given to him and have his heart brought to life, should show proper regard for his Lord and not delay the *salat* from its proper time and not permit himself any indulgence in doing so. Nor should he perform the *salat* alone when he is able to join a group prayer. Yet we see many people delaying their *salat* and praying by themselves when they are able to join a group. How evil is what they do.

We see them immersed in anxiety, sorrow, hardships and adversity. By Allah the source of what afflicts them is their laxity in the *deen*. We also notice that they see no difference between prayer in the first row and prayer in the last row. This is not because they do not know; it is just their lack of concern for the *deen*. They are not scrupulous about purity either. But the truth is that if anyone has any impurity on him, he has no *wudu*. If he has no *wudu*, he has no *salat*. And if he has no *salat* he has no good at all.

Shaykh al-Akhdari says in a moving passage in his small treatise on *salat*:

> There is an immense light in the *salat* that shines in the hearts of those who establish it and only comes to those who are humbly concentrated during it. So when you come to the *salat*, free your heart of this world and everything in it and busy yourself with concentrating on the presence of your Lord to whom your *salat* is addressed. You should know that the essence of the *salat* is humble concentration and submission to Allah by standing, bowing and prostrating before Him, and esteem and exaltation of Him by *takbir* (magnification), *tasbih* (glorification) and *dhikr* (remembrance).
>
> So safeguard your *salat*. It is the greatest of all the acts of worship. Do not allow Shaytan to play with your heart and distract you from it so that your heart is devastated and you are deprived of the sweetness of the lights of the *salat*. You must always strive to be humbly concentrated in it for it keeps you from indecency and wrongdoing according to the extent of your concentration in it. And ask Allah for help. He is the Best of Helpers.

Shaykh Zarruq quoted 'Umar ibn al-Khattab as writing to his governors:

> I think that the most important of your affairs is the prayer. Anyone who preserves it and perseveres in it will preserve other things. Whoever squanders it will squander other things. (The Muwatta)

It is clear from all this that *salat*, the physical act of prayer, which punctuates the day of every Muslim, truly is the cornerstone around which the life of every Muslim is built and its effect is incalculable. It puts the act of worship back where it belongs at the centre of human life and ensures the health of society as a whole. It gives people a correct perspective on existence so that they do not become totally engrossed in the life of this world. It is a continual reminder of the insubstantial nature of this life, that death is inevitable and that what follows it depends on the way we live and goes on forever. The acceptance of accountability implicit in this attitude makes people prone to live within the limits rather than wantonly transgress them. It creates a situation where people see that immediate self-gratification is not necessarily in their best interests and that generosity, patience and good character really do have benefits in them.

Zakat

...to pay the zakat

The literal meaning of the Arabic word *zakat* is growth, increase and purification. In the legal usage employed here it refers to the small percentage of surplus wealth of various types – namely certain kinds of agricultural produce, livestock, trade goods and monetary wealth – officially taken on an annual basis when they exceed specified amounts, which must then be distributed among particular categories of people in need. The reason the word is used is made clear by two references in the Qur'an where its connection with the original meaning is demonstrated: "*Take sadaqa from their wealth to purify and cleanse them*" (9:103) and "*But anything you give as zakat, seeking the Face of Allah – whoever does that will get back twice as much.*" (30:40) It is considered to be an act of worship just as prayer, fasting and pilgrimage.

The obligatory nature of *zakat* is specified in the Qur'an and the importance placed on it is shown by the fact that it is coupled with the command to do the prayer nearly thirty times.

Establish the prayer and pay zakat and obey the Messenger
  so that perhaps you may gain mercy. (24:54)

The men and women of the believers
  are friends of one another.
They command the right and forbid the wrong,

and establish the prayer and pay zakat,
and obey Allah and His Messenger.
They are the people Allah will have mercy on.
Allah is Almighty, All-Wise. (9:72)

Then the command comes:

Take sadaqa from their wealth
to purify and cleanse them. (9:104)

Another passage tells us categories to whom it may be given:

Collected sadaqa is for:
the poor,
the destitute,
those who collect it,
reconciling people's hearts,
freeing slaves,
those in debt,
spending in the way of Allah,
and travellers.
An obligation imposed by Allah.
Allah is All-Knowing, All-Wise. (9:60)

Note that *sadaqa*, which is widely thought only to mean voluntary charity, here refers to *zakat*.

THE PAYMENT OF ZAKAT

The types of wealth on which *zakat* must be paid are monetary wealth, crops and livestock. Monetary wealth refers to gold and silver, in whatever form they are held, and trade goods; crops comprise agricultural produce of the kind which can be stored for extended periods; and livestock refers to camels, cattle, sheep and goats.

Zakat became a legal obligation in the second year of Hijra. The evidence of its obligatory nature is the Book, the *Sunna* and the consensus of all the Muslims. There are certain conditions that make it obligatory and certain other conditions that make it valid. The conditions that make *zakat* obligatory are five in number.

- Islam: non-muslims do not pay *zakat*.
- Freedom: slaves do not pay *zakat*.
- *Nisab*: all types of wealth must reach a certain minimum amount before *zakat* becomes applicable.
- Ownership: *zakat* is only taken from wealth that is completely owned by the payer and completely at their disposal.
- A year's possession: monetary wealth and livestock must have been owned for a complete year before *zakat* is taken. This condition does not apply to agricultural produce.

There are five further conditions which apply to *zakat*.

- Intention: it must be remembered that *zakat* is an act of worship and requires a specific intention like all other acts of worship.
- Collection: *zakat* should be paid to a collector appointed by the leader of the Muslim community.
- Local distribution: *zakat* should be distributed among the community in which it is collected unless it is not possible to do so because none of the recipient categories exist there, in which case it may be sent elsewhere.
- Correct time: *zakat* should be paid promptly at, but not before, the time it falls due.
- Correct elements: *zakat* should be paid with the correct means according to the type of wealth in question: the right age and kind of animal in the case of livestock; the right quality of produce in the case of agricultural crops; and the right weight of gold and silver in the case of monetary wealth.

☆ ☆ ☆

Although it is true that the nature of people's wealth has changed in recent times and that for the vast majority only monetary wealth will come into the frame as far as *zakat* is concerned, there are still millions of Muslims throughout the world who are involved in agriculture and animal husbandry and so, without going into too much detail, it is appropriate to give the basic rules of *zakat* for these kinds of wealth. The quite complex specifications involved in the *zakat* on these types of wealth, which are outlined in many traditional books of Islamic law, show how essential it is to have officially appointed collectors who have the knowledge and experience necessary to ensure that correct and fair assessments are both made and carried out.

THE ZAKAT OF LIVESTOCK

As mentioned above, *zakat* must be paid on camels, cattle, sheep and goats provided that they reach the minimum number on which *zakat* is due. It makes no difference whether they are foddered or put out to grass nor whether they are used for milk, wool, meat, riding, as work animals or for any other purpose. As with monetary wealth, no *zakat* is taken unless the minimum zakatable number of animals has been in the possession of the owner for a full year. No *zakat* is due on horses unless they are kept or bred for trading purposes in which case they become classified as trading goods, and so enter the category of monetary wealth, and are assessed accordingly.

CAMELS

The minimum number of camels on which *zakat* is due is five. Between five and twenty-five, depending on the number, a certain number of sheep or goats must be paid as *zakat*. After twenty-five the *zakat* must be paid in camels of a particular age and sex depending on the number in the herd.

CATTLE

All types of cattle are considered together for *zakat* purposes.

The minimum number of cattle on which *zakat* is due is thirty. Thereafter *zakat* must be paid in cows of particular ages according to the number in the herd.

SHEEP AND GOATS

Sheep and goats are combined for *zakat* purposes. The minimum number on which *zakat* is due is forty, at which point one animal of a particular age must be paid as *zakat*. Another animal is due when the herd reaches one hundred and twenty in number and then more according to the size of the herd.

PARTNERSHIPS

In the case that animals are jointly owned by two or more partners *zakat* is owed on the whole flock or herd provided that each partner is a free Muslim and that their shares individually reach the minimum number on which *zakat* is due. The *zakat* should be shared between the partners according to the proportion which each owns of the whole flock or herd.

GENERAL

The official collector should visit each location at a given time each year in order to assess and take the *zakat* from every flock and herd. The animals taken as *zakat* should be of average size and in good condition. If the collector is late, *zakat* only has to be paid on the number of animals he finds, not on the number that may have been there when *zakat* fell due. If the owner has died and the animals have been inherited by a new owner he only pays *zakat* after the animals have been in his possession for a full year. It is not permitted for the owner of animals to assess his own *zakat* and give it out before the arrival of the collector, but if two years or more elapse without the collector coming, then the owner of the animals may assess and pay the *zakat* he owes to the appropriate recipients.

THE ZAKAT OF AGRICULTURAL PRODUCE

Various types of agricultural produce are subject to *zakat* and they are largely those foodstuffs which can be stored for extended periods. No *zakat* is due on fresh fruit and vegetables intended for immediate consumption. In agricultural *zakat* the *nisab* is the same for every type of produce, namely five *wasqs*. The *wasq* is a measure which corresponds to roughly a camel-load and is a measure of volume made up of sixty *sa's*. The *sa'* is equivalent to 2.035 litres so one *wasq* equals 122 litres. This means that the minimum amount of any type of agricultural produce on which *zakat* is due is 610 litres by volume. This is sometimes mistakenly expressed in terms of weight as 610 kgs. The problem is that the same volumes of different kinds of produce vary considerably in weight so that it is better to hold to the volumetric measure whenever possible.

The amount of *zakat* payable on agricultural produce varies according to how the land, in which the particular crop is being grown, is irrigated. The basic rule is that when the land is naturally irrigated, whether by rain or surface water such as rivers or springs, then one tenth of any crop which reaches the amount of the *nisab* is taken as *zakat*. When artificial means of irrigation have to be used, at the expense of the cultivator bringing water to the land, the *zakat* is only one twentieth of the crop. The *zakat* of agricultural produce should be assessed and collected by an officially appointed collector and none of a crop on which *zakat* is due may be consumed or sold until the *zakat* on it has been properly assessed.

CEREALS

Where cereals are concerned, *zakat* is assessed on the amount of actual grain which has been harvested after threshing has taken place. The *zakat* on cereals falls due once the crops have ripened in the field and should be paid immediately the harvesting process has been completed.

Certain grains are considered as forming a single category for *zakat* purposes, namely wheat, barley and rye. These are added together and if the combined quantity reaches the *nisab, zakat* is taken proportionally from each type of grain. Other types of grain are considered as forming separate categories and are not added together for *zakat* purposes, namely rice, sorghum, millet and maize, so that crops of these must each individually amount to the *nisab* before any *zakat* falls due on them.

PULSES

Lentils, chick-peas, peas, and various kinds of beans are also considered as forming a single category for *zakat* purposes and so crops of these grown by a single grower should be added together when calculating *zakat*. If the combined crop reaches the amount of the *nisab, zakat* is due on it and should be taken proportionally from each individual type of pulse.

OIL CROPS

Zakat is due on olives and various types of seed grown for their oil content. They are not added together, each being considered separate for *zakat* purposes. The *nisab* is calculated on the basis of the amount of actual fruit or seed harvested but the *zakat* should be paid in oil after pressing has taken place.

DATES AND RAISINS

Zakat must also be paid on dates and grapes when they are intended to be consumed as dried fruit. The *zakat* on them falls due when they are ripe on the branch but is, of course, paid after they have dried.

THE ZAKAT OF MONETARY WEALTH

THE PROBLEM OF PAPER MONEY

The last couple of centuries have witnessed a radical change in the way that wealth is viewed. Rather than being seen in terms of ownership of land as it used to be, and thus expressed largely in agricultural produce and livestock holdings, wealth is now seen in almost exclusively monetary terms. The whole subject is, however, from the *zakat* point of view, further complicated by the fact that the nature of money has also concurrently undergone a total transformation because of the fact that gold and silver have now been replaced by paper and electronic currencies. Since it is also clear that the *zakat* of monetary wealth may only be paid in gold and silver, it now becomes a question, given the current nature of money, of how that can, and indeed if it should, be brought about.

To start with it must be understood that, economically speaking, the current situation of the Muslims throughout the world, both because of their inextricable relationship with the openly usurious global economic system and also because of the nature of paper money itself, has clearly moved them into the realm of what is forbidden under Islamic law. This means that every Muslim should do everything in his power to change or disconnect from the present system because only then will it be possible to re-establish the pillar of *zakat* in a complete way and pay it correctly.

It is necessary, however, to start from the present situation. The change that has taken place in the nature of money must be faced and a way found to enable *zakat* to be paid in the light of the type of currencies at present in existence. The great Egyptian scholar Shaykh 'Illish was asked about paying *zakat* on paper money when it first appeared among the Muslims. He issued a judgement declaring that *zakat* should not be paid on it, viewing it logically as numbered tokens worth in reality no more than the value of the paper they are printed on. And there have been many eminent scholars since who have reached the same conclusion. However, it is well known that paper money was originally intended to directly represent certain specific amounts of gold and silver and, if that view of it is taken, then banknotes are in reality acknowledgements of a debt owed by a bank to the bearer of the note.

From the standpoint of *zakat* there are two difficulties in taking this position. The first is that while this specific gold/silver equivalence was the initial intention of paper money, it

The Natural Form of Man

is clearly no longer the case since paper currencies have long since given up any pretence of being tied to their original direct connection with gold and silver coinage.

The second is that while it is true that creditors must pay *zakat* on debts owed to them they do not have to do so until the debt has been repaid, since, although they own the money, they do not have full use of it until it returns to their possession. But in the case of paper money no such restriction exists because the possessors of the banknotes have full use of the value they represent, by their use of them as a medium of exchange in the country in which they live, even though they do not have possession of it in real terms.

So for *zakat* purposes it is better to view paper money as being like bond certificates whose value is guaranteed by the government. This does not in fact legitimise their use as a medium of exchange by Muslims, since there is no way under the laws of Islam that such financial instruments can be employed to replace gold and silver coinage as money, but it does provide a way of understanding their usage and of making it possible to assess them for *zakat* purposes. This is because, although they are forbidden by Islamic law, they have been imposed on people by force as being the sole means of exchange whereby they are able to conduct all the financial transactions necessary for their lives. This brings the legal principle of *darura* (unavoidable necessity) into play, whereby the forbidden becomes temporarily permissible if it is a question of preserving life. On this basis alone the use of paper money has gained a temporary, but extremely reluctant, permissibility for the Muslim community.

Although paper money may be used and assessed for *zakat* purposes on this basis, that still does not make it permissible to pay any *zakat* owed in any other form than the actual gold and silver which Islamic law requires since, firstly, there is no evidence that anything else has ever been legally acceptable and, secondly, there is no difficulty in obtaining the gold and silver necessary to fulfil the obligation, especially now that prophetically sanctioned gold dinars and silver dirhams are becoming increasingly available throughout the world.

THE NISAB FOR THE ZAKAT OF MONETARY WEALTH

The *nisab* for monetary wealth in silver is two hundred dirhams and in gold it is twenty dinars. Records of the respective weights of the silver dirham and the gold dinar have been kept from the earliest times and it is known that a dirham weighed the equivalent of 2.965 grammes and a dinar the equivalent of 4.235 grammes on the basis of a ratio of seven dinars to ten dirhams by weight. This means that the *nisab* in terms of silver is 593 grammes or 20.92 ounces and in terms of gold it is 84.7 grammes or 2.99 ounces.

ZAKAT ON SAVINGS

In the light of the above it is, therefore, appropriate for *zakat* to be taken from wealth held in paper currencies, whether in the form of actual banknotes, bank accounts, or any other kinds of savings accounts, provided they amount to at least the value of the *nisab* and have been continuously in the possession of their owner for at least a year. If that is the case then one fortieth or two and a half percent of their value must be paid in gold or silver as *zakat*. In view of the current extremely low price of silver it would seem better to take the gold *nisab* for *zakat* purpose, and scholars have given judgement to this effect. Their argument is that the *nisab* reflects to some degree the amount of money equivalent to a year's provision, and this is more closely reflected in the price of the gold *nisab*. But whichever *nisab* is chosen *zakat* should be paid in the metal whose *nisab* is selected, so that if *zakat* is calculated using the silver *nisab* it must be paid in silver and if *zakat* is calculated using the gold *nisab* it must be paid in gold.

ZAKAT ON TRADE GOODS

Trade goods are also considered by Islamic law as monetary wealth on which *zakat* is due. Trade goods are all goods which have been purchased or acquired or manufactured with the primary intention of resale. There are basically two kinds of trade goods.

The first are the kind of goods which are bought with future resale in mind but which may stay in the possession of the purchaser for a considerable period before he sells them. If the value of such an item amounts to the *nisab* or more and it remains in your possession for at least a year then *zakat* should be paid in gold or silver on the price received when it is sold.

The second type of trade goods are those goods subject to constant turnover, such as the stock of a shop or a market stall or any other kind of trading or manufacturing business. When someone has such stock, *zakat* is assessed on the basis of a regular annual valuation, on a particular selected date, of the stock, liquid capital in hand and debts owed. The valuation is made on the current market price of the goods concerned. If the stock and accumulated capital combined, minus debts owed, amount to the *nisab* or more, then one fortieth of their value must be paid in gold or silver as *zakat*.

Debts

There are two kinds of debts, those you owe to other people and those other people owe to you, and both kinds of debts have a bearing on the *zakat* of monetary wealth.

If you owe money to others, then the amount you owe is subtracted from the amount of monetary wealth you possess before your *zakat* is assessed so that, for instance, if you possess monetary wealth adding up to more than the *nisab* but when your outstanding debts are taken into account the amount is reduced to less than the *nisab*, then you have no *zakat* to pay. If, however, you have disposable assets, which are not liable to *zakat* but which could be sold to pay off all or some of what you owe, then your debt is considered to have been reduced by the amount of the combined market value of those assets.

In the case of agricultural produce and livestock, debt is not taken into account when assessing the amount of *zakat* owed.

If money amounting to the value of the *nisab* or more is owed to you and remains outstanding for a year or more, you owe *zakat* on it but do not have to pay that *zakat* until the loan is repaid to you.

BUSINESS INVESTMENTS

Investments are basically of two kinds, those whose primary purpose is to produce profit through resale and those whose primary purpose is to produce income. They are treated for *zakat* purposes in a similar way to trade goods. So that if, for instance, you own a property company whose principal activity is buying and selling houses then your whole property portfolio is viewed as turnover stock which should be valued annually and *zakat* paid on the total value. If, however, your main intention is to produce income through letting out the properties you own, then you will only pay *zakat* on the price you receive if and when you sell one of those properties. The basic principle applies that *zakat* is only due on goods or property acquired with the intention of resale in mind.

PERSONAL PROPERTY

No *zakat* is owed on personal property such as houses, furniture, household goods, transport or land which are regularly used by you and your family and not intended for trade. The same applies to gold and silver jewellery which are regularly worn and not intended for investment or trading purposes. The same also applies to tools you own which you use to earn your living and, in the case of a business, buildings and plant used in the carrying on of the business. As mentioned earlier, however, the value of disposable personal assets which could be sold to pay debts is set against outstanding debts when *zakat* is being assessed.

GENERAL

This contains all the general principles appertaining to the *zakat* of monetary wealth and they seem fairly straightforward on the surface. What you find, however, when you go into the details of people's individual circumstances, is that there are endless anomalies and exceptions and it would be impossible to cover all of them. This is a further reason why it is indispensable to have officially appointed *zakat* assessors and collectors with a thorough knowledge of all the laws of *zakat* and experience in dealing with *zakat* in the light of the many and varied financial circumstances which people face in the world today.

THE RECIPIENTS OF ZAKAT

There are eight categories of people to whom the collected *zakat* must be distributed by the leader of the Muslims. Allah, may He be exalted and glorified, lists them for us in the Qur'an when He says: *"Collected sadaqa is for: the poor, the destitute, those who collect it, reconciling people's hearts, freeing slaves, those in debt, spending in the way of Allah, and travellers."* (9:60)

THE POOR

The poor are considered to be those Muslims who have some means of support but not sufficient to cover their needs, so they may have a job or a business, and could even own property such as the house in which they live, but their income is not enough to pay the basic living expenses of themselves and their families. Such people are entitled to be given enough *zakat* to bring their income up to a level which enables them to meet their basic needs. This may well be the case with a merchant whose capital and stock reach the amount of the *nisab*. In that case he must pay whatever *zakat* he owes but will also be entitled to receive *zakat* on the basis of his personal financial situation.

THE DESTITUTE

The destitute are Muslims who have no property and no income whatsoever. There are, of course, many reasons which might bring this situation about. It might be due to a calamity that has befallen them or a disability which prevents them from earning or they may be people who have some property to which for some reason they temporarily have no access. Students might also fall into this category if their studies genuinely prevent them from earning and they have no other means of support.

THE COLLECTORS

The collectors and the distributors of *zakat* are also entitled to a share of it. Such men must, however, be Muslims, free men, upright and just, and well versed in all the prescriptions of Islamic law relative to the assessment and collection of *zakat*. This applies even if they have other means since it is in the nature of a salary for the work they do. No *zakat*, however, may be given to those who are placed in the position of being its custodians. They must be paid from other sources. Nor may the *zakat* collectors take their pay from the *zakat* they themselves collect, but it must be given them from other *zakat*.

PEOPLE WHOSE HEARTS ARE TO BE RECONCILED

This applies firstly to people who have just become Muslim or are on the point of doing so and who may be strengthened or swayed by help from *zakat* funds, and secondly to non-Muslims who are friendly towards the Muslims and who can be of some help in a war situation. This permission, which is an exception to the general rule, is dependent upon close examination of the circumstances of those involved because *zakat* grants should only be made to non-Muslims when there is real necessity for their services or when there is a certainty of their sincere desire to become Muslims.

FREEING SLAVES

Zakat may be employed to help Muslim slaves to buy their freedom. Slaves freed by this means remain under the clientage of the Muslim community.

THOSE IN DEBT

Zakat may be given to an individual to pay his debts, as long as these are not debts connected with the *deen*. This applies even to debtors who have died. *Zakat* to debtors is conditional on them already having handed over to their creditors all the spare money and property in their possession.

IN THE WAY OF ALLAH

This category is generally considered to be confined to those fighting *jihad* to enable them to mount and equip themselves properly. Such grants may be made to fighting men even if they are well off. No part of the *zakat* may, however, be used for the construction and upkeep of fortifications, nor for works entailed by a defensive war, nor for the construction of warships, nor for the building of mosques or any other public works.

TRAVELLERS

Zakat may also be used for the support and repatriation of travellers, providing they are free Muslims, who have need of such help. This is dependent on them not being able to find anyone who can lend them what they require.

GENERAL

What is clear from the above categories is that *zakat* acts in Muslim society as the helper of last resort, a kind of social safety net. The recipients of *zakat* are all people who have no access to any other source of help in their particular situation. It is important to understand that *zakat* is not charity. Private giving and the establishment of *awqaf* (endowments) take care of all the ordinary charitable needs of the Muslim community. *Zakat* is there to see to the needs of all those who have nowhere else to go. This is another reason why it is important that *zakat* should be collected communally and distributed locally since it is only communally that sufficient funds can be gathered and efficiently distributed and only on a local level that people's real needs can be properly recognised and taken care of.

A political leader is necessary in each Muslim community to oversee the collection and distribution of *zakat* in each locality. Normally some of the *zakat*, although not a fixed share, is allocated to the collectors and then the needs of the community's poor and destitute taken care of, and then those of the other categories when and where appropriate. The decision about this rests in the hands of the political leader of the Muslims and so such a leader must exist in every community to enable *zakat* to be distributed properly. Imam Malik puts the whole matter of distribution very clearly in the *Muwatta* when he says in the *Book of Zakat* in the section on those entitled to receive *zakat*:

> The position with us concerning the dividing up of *zakat* is that it is up to the individual judgement of the man in charge. Whichever categories of people are in most need and are most numerous are given preference, according to how the man in charge sees fit. It is possible that this may change after a year, or two, or more, but it is always those who are in need and are most numerous that are given preference, whatever category they may belong to. This is what I have seen done by people of knowledge with whom I am satisfied.

ZAKAT AL-FITR

Zakat al-fitr is fundamentally different from the types of *zakat* which have been looked at up to now. The *zakat* looked at so far has been a tax on superfluous wealth whereas *zakat al-fitr* is a tax on the individual, in which the amount of wealth they have plays no part. The two types of *zakat* are also completely independent of one another. Payment of the *zakat* on your wealth does not absolve you from paying *zakat al-fitr* and payment of *zakat al-fitr* does not absolve you from having to pay *zakat* on your wealth if you have sufficient to warrant it.

WHO PAYS ZAKAT AL-FITR

Zakat al-fitr was imposed by the Prophet ﷺ as an obligatory tax to be paid by or on behalf of every Muslim at the end of Ramadan, no matter what their age, sex, economic circumstances or social status. A man must pay for all those for whose upkeep he is normally responsible – wives, children, slaves or other dependents. People who live alone must, of course, pay for themselves individually. The point is that *zakat al-fitr* is owed by every single Muslim at the conclusion of Ramadan and its importance is made clear by the fact that in one hadith the Prophet 🕮 made the acceptance of the fast by Allah dependent upon its payment.

THE AMOUNT AND FORM OF PAYMENT OF ZAKAT AL-FITR

The amount owed by every individual as *zakat al-fitr* is one *sa‘* of the staple food of the people in the locality where they live. As was made clear above, the *sa‘* is a measure equivalent to just over two litres, so in a place where the staple food is bread the *zakat al-fitr* is that quantity of wheat per person, where it is rice, then it is rice, and so on. Where various foods are eaten then it could take the form of whatever grain or pulse or dried fruit are acceptable in that area.

THE TIME OF PAYMENT AND DISTRIBUTION OF ZAKAT AL-FITR

Zakat al-fitr falls due on the last evening of Ramadan after the *Eid* has been announced and is best discharged before going to the *Eid* prayer the following morning, although there is no harm in paying it after going to the prayer. It is also permitted to pay it somewhat early during the last couple of days of Ramadan. It should be given to people in the community who are known to be poor. Unlike other types of *zakat* it can be distributed individually and does not have to be centrally collected, although there is no harm in doing that.

JIZYA

The *jizya* is a tax levied on all non-Muslim adult males living under Muslim rule. Like *zakat* it has implications which go far beyond its primary function as a source of revenue for the Muslim government. Sanction for it, indeed the command to collect it, comes directly from the Qur'an when Allah says in *Surat at-Tawba*, "*Fight those of the people who were given the Book who do not believe in Allah and the Last Day and do not forbid what Allah and His Messenger have forbidden and do not take as their deen the deen of Truth, until they pay the jizya with their own hands in a state of complete submission."* (9:28)

The need for the Muslims to understand the importance of *jizya* as a legal principle has never been more pressing than at present. It accomplishes two vital functions at one and the same time. It makes it clear beyond any doubt that Muslim governance can only be based on the worship of Allah alone and acceptance of Allah's laws as outlined in His Book and clarified and expounded through the *Sunna* of His Messenger ﷺ. It categorically precludes the substitution of any other premise or constitution as the statutory foundation of any Muslim society. By doing this it deals a death blow to secularism, which is overtly or covertly the basis of virtually all government in the world today.

The idea of secularism was first introduced at the end of the seventeenth century precisely in order to remove Divinely revealed law from the statute books with the primary purpose of allowing financiers free rein in their eventually successful bid to achieve world domination through the employment of previously Divinely forbidden usurious financial techniques. The justifying rationale behind the move towards the secularisation of government was that it would make adherents of every religious faith equal under the law, but what it really entailed, apart from divorcing government from its last connection with Divine Revelation, was making every religion essentially the same and, by doing that, in fact denying all religious truth.

Jizya, on the other hand, puts everything in its right place, affirming the supremacy of Islam as the final Divine Revelation for all mankind but permitting the continued existence of previous religions in the subservient position which their supersedure by Islam demands. The only way to order human society is in accordance with the extent to which people acknowledge their Creator and agree to live by the laws He has prescribed for them which alone can ensure justice and balance for the human race.

Allah makes the position abundantly plain a few *ayats* after his command to take *jizya* when He says in conclusion to that particular passage, *"It is He who sent His Messenger with guidance and the Deen of Truth to exalt it over every other deen, even though the idolaters hate it."* (9:33)

THE PAYMENT OF JIZYA

Jizya is a tax imposed on all people of other religions who want to live under Muslim rule without accepting Islam. The amount of the tax is four dinars which must be paid annually by all adult males. Women, children, slaves, lunatics, paupers, monks, hermits and the sick are exempt from *jizya*. It must be taken in a manner which shows the submission of the payer which means it may not be gathered collectively but must be paid by each man individually to the Muslim authorities. If someone is in straitened circumstances the amount of his *jizya* may be reduced at the discretion of the Muslim leader.

Ironically, people who regard the imposition of the *jizya* as intolerable have long ago accepted to pay vastly greater amounts of money in taxation enduring more serious humiliation in the process.

In return for the payment of *jizya* the property and lives of non-Muslims under Muslim rule are protected and they are permitted to own property and carry on trade within the limits of Islamic law, and they may not be enslaved.

Sawm/Fasting

to fast Ramadan…

THE MAIN REFERENCE to fasting in the Qur'an occurs in the clear instructions about Ramadan which are to be found in *Surat al-Baqara*:

You who believe! fasting is prescribed for you,
*   as it was prescribed for those before you –*
*   so that hopefully you will be godfearing –*
for a specified number of days.
But any of you who are ill or on a journey
*   should fast a number of other days.*
For those who are able to fast,
*   their reparation is to feed the poor.*
And if someone does good of his own accord,
*   it is better for him.*
But that you should fast is better for you,
*   if you only knew.*

The month of Ramadan is the one in which the Qur'an
*   was sent down as guidance for mankind,*
*   with Clear Signs containing*
*   guidance and discrimination.*
Any of you who are resident for the month should fast it.

But any of you who are ill or on a journey
  should fast a number of other days.
  Allah desires ease for you;
He does not desire difficulty for you.
  You should complete the number of days
    and proclaim Allah's greatness
      for the guidance He has given you
      so that hopefully you will be thankful.

If My slaves ask you about Me, I am near.
  I answer the call of the caller when he calls on Me.
They should therefore respond to Me and believe in Me
  so that hopefully they will be rightly guided.

On the night of the fast it is lawful for you
    to have sexual relations with your wives.
  They are clothing for you and you for them.
Allah knows that you have been betraying yourselves
  and He has turned towards you and excused you.
Now you may have sexual intercourse with them
  and seek what Allah has written for you.
Eat and drink until you can clearly discern
  the white thread from the black thread of the dawn,
    then fulfil the fast until the night appears.
But do not have sexual intercourse with them
  while you are in retreat in the mosques.
These are Allah's limits, so do not go near them.
Thus does Allah make His Signs clear to people
  so that hopefully they will be godfearing. (2:182-186)

There are also, however, many statements from the Prophet ﷺ which speak of fasting and its benefits. Among them are:

Abu Hurayra said that the Messenger of Allah ﷺ said, "Allah, the Mighty and Exalted has said, 'Every action of the son of Adam is for himself except for fasting. It is Mine and I repay it.' Fasting is a shield. When someone is fasting, he should not have sexual relations nor quarrel. If someone fights him or insults him, he should say, 'I am fasting'. By the One in whose hand the self of Muhammad is, the changed breath in the mouth of the faster is more fragrant to Allah than the scent of musk. The faster experiences two joys: when he breaks his fast he rejoices and when he meets his Lord he rejoices in his fasting." (Al-Bukhari, Muslim, an-Nasa'i)

In one variant of al-Bukhari, it includes the words of Allah transmitted by the Prophet, may Allah bless him and grant him peace:

"He has left his food and drink and appetites for My sake. Fasting is Mine and I repay it. Any other good deed I repay with ten like it."

In a variant of Muslim:

"Every action of the son of Adam is multiplied. A good action receives from ten to seven hundred times. Allah Almighty said, 'Fasting is Mine and I repay it. He leaves his appetites and food for My sake.' The faster experiences two joys: a joy when he breaks his fast and a joy when he meets his Lord. The changed breath in the mouth of the faster is more fragrant to Allah than the scent of musk."

Also:

Sahl ibn Sa'd reported that the Prophet ﷺ said, "There is a gate in the Garden called *ar-Rayyan* which those who fast will enter on the Day of Rising, and none but they will enter it. It will be said, 'Where are the fasters?' They will stand up and none but they will enter it. When they have entered it, it will be closed and no one else will enter it." (Ahmad, al-Bukhari, Muslim)

Abu Hurayra reported that the Messenger of Allah ﷺ said, "Anyone who prays in Ramadan motivated by belief and in expectation of reward will be forgiven his past wrong actions." (Al-Bukhari, Muslim, at-Tirmidhi, an-Nasa'i, Ibn Majah, Abu Dawud)

Abu Hurayra reported that the Messenger of Allah ﷺ said, "When Ramadan comes, the gates of the Garden are opened, the gates of the Fire are closed and the shaytans are chained up." (Al-Bukhari, Muslim)

Abu Hurayra reported that the Messenger of Allah ﷺ said, "Fast when you see it (the new moon) and break the fast when you see it. If it is cloudy, then complete Sha'ban as thirty days." (Al-Bukhari, Muslim, an-Nasa'i)

In a variant of Muslim:

"If it is cloudy, you must fast thirty days."

Other hadiths have:

Ibn 'Abbas said, "The Prophet ﷺ was the most generous of people, and he was even more generous during Ramadan when Jibril met him. Jibril used to meet him every night in Ramadan until it was over and the Prophet ﷺ would go through the Qur'an with him. The Messenger of Allah ﷺ was more generous with good things than the loosed wind." (Al-Bukhari, Muslim)

'A'isha said, "When the last ten days of Ramadan started, the Messenger of Allah ﷺ used to pray during the night, wake up his family and intensify his efforts." (Muslim)

Abu Hurayra reported that the Prophet ﷺ said, "Allah does not require someone who does not abandon lies and acting by them while fasting to abandon his food and drink." (Ahmad, al-Bukhari, Abu Dawud, at-Tirmidhi, Ibn Majah)

THE LEGAL RULINGS CONCERNING FASTING

The Arabic word for fasting, *sawm*, means literally "to refrain from" and as a technical term in Islamic law it signifies refraining from food, drink and sex during the daylight hours between dawn and sunset. Fasting in this way is obligatory for every Muslim over the age of puberty during the twenty-nine or thirty days of the lunar month of Ramadan each year which begins with the first sighting of the new moon at the beginning of the month of Ramadan and ends with the first sighting of the new moon at the beginning of the following month of Shawwal.

It is essential to make an intention for the obligatory fast of Ramadan. This intention must be made before dawn on the first day and, according to the Maliki school, one intention is sufficient for the whole month unless the fast is broken because of menstruation, travelling or illness in which case a new intention must be made before recommencing the fast. According to some schools it is necessary to renew the intention before dawn each day. If Ramadan begins and you do not realise it has begun and start the day eating, you start fasting the moment you find out and must make up another day after the end of the month.

As has been said, the fast lasts from first light until the sun has set. It is *sunna* to delay *suhur*, the pre-dawn meal, until the very last part of the night, while of course being careful not to eat after dawn has actually arrived; and it is also *sunna* to break the fast as soon as possible after sunset, preferably with dates and milk or water.

Every Muslim beyond the age of puberty is required to fast. Pregnant women and nursing mothers are permitted to break the fast if they fear for the health of their babies or for their own health but they must make up the fast when they are able to and also, in the case of nursing mothers, feed one person for every day they missed. It is permitted to break the fast because of travelling, provided that the journey is long enough to allow the prayer to be shortened, or because of illness, but in both cases you must make up any days you miss. If you fail to make up any of these days before the next Ramadan comes you must also feed people as well for the days you failed to make up. If you break the fast out of forgetfulness or by accident you must make up a day and also continue to fast the rest of the day once you realise.

Another condition of the fast is that sexual intercourse is forbidden during the hours of fasting and this is generally extended to include any sexual activity or sexual stimulation which might lead to sexual fulfilment. This is something people have to be particularly careful about in this day and age when sexually explicit material is so prolific and easily accessible and in some instances practically unavoidable. Sexual emission in the waking state during the hours of fasting incurs the penalty of *kaffara* in the same way as intentionally eating and drinking does. The *kaffara* for breaking the fast is feeding sixty poor people or setting free a slave or fasting for two consecutive months. Sexual relations between husband and wife are, of course, permitted during the hours of darkness.

One of the extra practices particular to Ramadan is the confirmed *sunna* of *tarawih*, the night prayers done behind the imam after *Salat al-Isha*. This is a practice containing much benefit for those who participate in it, not least of which is hearing the recitation of a lot of the Book of Allah.

The month of fasting begins and ends with the physical sighting of the new moon. According to what has come down to us, this must be confirmed in clear weather by a general sighting of many people, or if it is cloudy by at least two reliable witnesses, who then convey the news to the Muslim leader of the locality concerned who then, in turn, announces the beginning or end of the fast to the community at large. It is clear that the beginning and end of Ramadan in any given locality is a political decision made by the local Muslim leader on the basis of the information he receives about the sighting of the moon. This goes without saying in countries where most or all the people are Muslims but can lead to problems in a situation where Muslims live under non-Muslim rule.

Finally it is worth repeating the words of the Prophet ﷺ when he said that many people get nothing from their fast but hunger and nothing from their night prayers but tiredness, which make it clear that the business of fasting extends far beyond mere abstention from food, drink and sex. The tongue must be guarded and, indeed, all the limbs, from anything which will detract from the fast and all Muslims should honour and respect the great gift of Ramadan which, of His limitless generosity, Allah, blessed is He and exalted, has blessed them with, so that the words of the Prophet 卿, "Anyone who fasts Ramadan with belief and with anticipation of reward for doing it is forgiven all his previous wrong actions," will become in every way a reality for them. (Ahmad, al-Bukhari, Muslim, at-Tirmidhi, Abu Dawud, an-Nasa'i, Ibn Majah)

GENERAL REMARKS ABOUT FASTING

The great Companion Salman 卿 said that the Messenger of Allah 卿 spoke on the last day of Sha'ban (the month before Ramadan) and said:

> O people! A great and blessed month has come to you – a month in which there is a night which is better than a thousand months; a month in which Allah has made it obligatory to fast and in which He has made standing in prayer during the night a voluntary action. Anyone who draws near to Allah during it by means of a voluntary good action is like someone who performs one of the obligatory actions outside it and performing an obligatory action during it is equivalent to performing seventy obligatory actions at any other time. It is the month of steadfast patience and the reward for steadfast patience is the Garden. It is the month of generous giving and the month in which a believer's provision is increased. If someone gives someone fasting something with which to break their fast, that will bring him forgiveness for his wrong actions and remove him from the Fire, and he will have the same reward as the one he feeds without that diminishing their reward in any way. (Sahih Ibn Khuzayma)

There are two aspects to Ramadan. The first is the activity of fasting and the second is the nature of the time itself. There is no spiritual tradition which does not practise fasting in one form or another. Fasting is, in fact, a defining human practice. Any other healthy hungry creature than a human being will, if offered food it likes, automatically consume it. Only a human being is able, by an act of will, to abstain from eating in those circumstances. This makes it a very special act of worship which is very highly rewarded by Allah when it is done for His sake. There are many benefits to be gained from it, not least of which are the well-attested medical ones – there is no doubt that it is excellent for our bodily health. However, perhaps the greatest benefit lies in the fact that by not eating and drinking when we want to we break one of the fundamental and basic links which imprison us in this lower world.

Our primary and primal connection with the world is made when we start feeding at our mother's breast and this is continued through the eating patterns we form throughout our childhood and into adult life. The effect of breaking this pattern is to open up to us access to direct knowledge of the substructure of our own selves and beyond that to the presence of our All-Providing Lord. Shaykh Abdalqadir as-Sufi talks of the highest possibilities opened up to us by the process of fasting when discussing it in his seminal work, *The Way of Muhammad*. He says:

> ...the whole self-pattern is opened up for the faster to see. ... He is aware that any constancy of self he imagined he had was merely a surface illusion buoyed up by habit pattern and behaviour structure designed to give an illusion of solidity. He begins to know himself as a shuddering, evanescent, melting, moving reality ... As the veils lift the Light becomes brighter. ... Fasting is the opening onto the Reality; it is the melting away of the solid, the dispersal of the cloud-body and the appearance of the sun-spirit.

Perhaps this goes some way towards explaining the meaning of the hadith of the Prophet 🕌 when he said:

> Every good action of the son of Adam is multiplied by ten to seven hundred times. Allah says: "Except fasting. It is mine and I repay it Myself. The faster abandons his food and drink for My sake." The faster has two delights: delight when he breaks his fast and delight when he meets his Lord. (Ahmad, Muslim, an-Nasa'i, Ibn Majah)

There is no doubt that Ramadan is a special time; every Muslim knows this. It is somehow qualitatively different from every other time. This is quite independent from the activity of fasting. It is not that fasting makes Ramadan different, it is rather that Allah has made it obligatory to fast during it so that the Muslims will gain the maximum benefit from its specialness as a time. Allah, may He be exalted, has made it the setting for a great secret, the *Laylatu'l-Qadr* – that night which the Qur'an tells us is better than a thousand months – and for that reason the Prophet 🕌 had chosen it for his retreats before his Prophethood began. Then, on that night, the great opening occurred; the beyond-time and the in-time intersected; the revelation of Allah's Book began. As several commentators of the Qur'an have pointed out, a thousand months is more or less the life-span of a human being; in other words, all the experience of time that any of us can have. So what is being indicated by the description in the Qur'an of the *Laylatu'l-Qadr* is that it is out of time, a moment in the year when a window opens onto timelessness, when human beings somehow have access to the very Presence of Allah.

It is this moment which permeates the whole month so that in it the Gates of the Garden are open and a faint resonance of the soft and fragrant breezes from them waft down into this world; and the satans which usually crowd in on people, poking at them and making it difficult for them to remember Allah and act rightly, are chained up, giving their hearts a welcome taste of ease and freedom. This is why good action is so highly rewarded during the month of Ramadan, as the hadith tells us. However, as with all good news there is an element of warning mixed in with it which is that it is extremely precious and Muslims cannot afford to waste any of it. It is important to take from it the maximum possible advantage because it is a time in which a benefit can be gained whose effects can last throughout the whole year which follows.

Hajj/Pilgrimage

to make the Pilgrimage to the House...
if you are able to do so

The Hajj is referred to several times in the Qur'an and in considerable detail:

Perform the Hajj and 'umra for Allah.
  If you are forcibly prevented,
      make whatever sacrifice is feasible.
But do not shave your heads until the sacrificial animal
      has reached the place of sacrifice.
If any of you are ill or have a head injury, the expiation
      is fasting or sadaqa or sacrifice
          when you are safe and well again.
Anyone who comes out of ihram between 'umra and Hajj
      should make whatever sacrifice is feasible.
For any one who cannot, there is three days' fast on Hajj
      and seven on your return – that is ten in all.
That is for anyone whose family does not live near
      the Masjid al-Haram.
Have taqwa of Allah and know
      that Allah is fierce in retribution.

The Hajj takes place during certain well-known months.
      If anyone undertakes the obligation of Hajj in them,

there must be no sexual intercourse, no wrongdoing,
  nor any quarrelling during Hajj.
Whatever good you do, Allah knows it.
    Take provision;
      but the best provision
        is taqwa of Allah.
So have taqwa of Me, people of intelligence!

There is nothing wrong in seeking bounty from your Lord.
  When you pour down from Arafat,
    remember Allah at the Sacred Landmark.
Remember Him because He has guided you,
  even though before this you were astray.

Then press on from where the people press on
  and ask Allah's forgiveness.
Allah is Ever-Forgiving, Most Merciful. (2:195-198)

Safa and Marwa are among the Landmarks of Allah,
  so anyone who goes on Hajj to the House or does 'umra
incurs no wrong in going back and forth between them.
  If anyone spontaneously does good,
Allah is All-Thankful, All-Knowing. (2:157)

And We located the position of the House for Ibrahim:
  'Do not associate anything with Me
and purify My House for those who circle it,
  and those who stand and bow and prostrate.

Announce the Hajj to mankind.
  They will come to you on foot
    and on every sort of lean animal,
  coming by every distant road
so that they can be present at what will profit them
  and invoke Allah's name on particular days
    over livestock He has provided for them.
Eat of them and feed those who are poor and in need.

*Then they should end their state of self-neglect
and fulfil their vows and circle the Ancient House.'*
(22:24-27)

GENERAL REMARKS ABOUT THE *HAJJ*

The *Hajj* is unique. There is nothing that happens on our planet that is in any way comparable to it. It represents the only truly global pattern of human social behaviour. If someone out in space were to observe the surface of the earth as a whole over a period of years, indeed of centuries, they would see many localised patterns of movement by human beings. They would see cities filling up and emptying out on a daily basis as people go to and from their places of work. They would probably notice within the continent of Europe a seasonal movement backwards and forwards between North and South as people head for the sun for their summer holidays. But in the main the movement of people about the surface of the earth would appear to be completely random to an outside observer and it would seem that there was no real cohesive human activity involving the whole human race. Just one thing would belie this conclusion.

At a certain time every year people would start, at first by ones and twos and gradually in ever increasing numbers, to move towards and gather together in one particular arid spot on the earth's surface. If the observer had very sophisticated equipment he would see the growing gathering going round and round in circles about one central point and then backwards and forwards between two adjacent points. Then on a clearly pre-specified date the whole mass of gathered people would be seen to move into a nearby valley and the following day to stream across the desert and remain stationary there for several hours. They would then return to the valley from which they had set out and, after a couple of days, they would start to disperse and return to all the places, near and far, from which they had originally come. Our observer in space would certainly conclude that this was the one discernible phenomenon which tied together the whole human race and the only global pattern of human activity. From our necessarily limited earthbound human perspective it is all too easy to lose sight of this universal aspect of the great institution of *Hajj* and to forget what a truly magnificent thing it is.

Another aspect that tends to be lost sight of is the ancientness of the *Hajj* and the fact that by participating in it Muslims are carrying on an unbroken tradition which has continued uninterruptedly from the very dawn of human history. It is at least six thousand years since the Prophet Ibrahim instituted the rites of *Hajj* centred on the House he built in the valley of Makka and it has been going on in that place year by year ever since that time. And there is compelling evidence from other parts of the world, including in Europe and all over the British Isles, that similar gatherings, involving circles and straight lines, were taking place in even earlier times. So when Muslims go on *Hajj* they are taking part in a series of rituals that have been an integral part of human existence since well before the beginning of recorded history. In fact they may well be the only surviving link, connecting human beings back to their first forefather Adam and the beginning of the human race.

THE RITES OF *HAJJ*

Those intending to do the *Hajj* should enter the state of *ihram,* making a clear intention for undertaking the *Hajj,* after performing an obligatory or voluntary prayer. You go into *ihram* or take on *ihram* when you pass a particular point known as the *miqat* on your way to do the *Hajj.* Once you have done so, certain normally permitted things become forbidden to you. Men may wear no sewn garments and may not cover their heads. Women wear ordinary clothing and may not cover their faces. While in *ihram,* it is forbidden to hunt game, to kill lice or any similar insects or, indeed, any animal except specific dangerous ones, to have sexual contact of any kind, to fight or quarrel, to contract or perform a marriage, to shave or comb or scratch your head or do anything which is likely to remove hair from your head or body, to cut the nails, to use perfume or beautify the body in any way. It is *sunna* to have a *ghusl* before going into *ihram* and to pray two *rak'ats* when you have done so and it is the time when your *Hajj* begins and when your formal intention to perform *Hajj* should be made.

Just as with the *takbirat al-ihram* in the prayer you cut yourself off from the world and devote your attention to Allah for the length of the prayer, so with the *ihram* of the *Hajj* you cut yourself off from the normal preoccupations of your life and devote yourself to the service of Allah in the way that He has prescribed until your *Hajj* is concluded. It is as if during the whole time you are in *ihram* your body no longer has importance and it is only your connection with your Lord that matters. You have to eat and do *wudu* but apart from that you forget about your body and its appearance altogether. It is the only time when letting yourself go is obligatory and normal grooming forbidden.

There are four *miqats*, depending on which direction you approach Makka from. These days, when many people going on *Hajj* fly directly into Jeddah, which is already beyond all the *miqats*, the usual practice is to change into the clothing of *ihram* before boarding the plane and to remake the intention for the *Hajj* when you fly over the *miqat* point. From this point the precluded activities we mentioned become *haram* – forbidden.

After entering *ihram* you should recite the expression known as the *talbiya* which begins: *labbayk Allahumma labbayk* (At Your service, O Allah, at Your service). This should be repeated periodically throughout the journey, particularly after the obligatory *salat*, at sunrise, when groups of people are met, and at other appropriate moments, without going to excess. When you enter Makka you should stop reciting the *talbiya* until after you have completed the opening rites of *tawaf* and *sa'y* and then resume it until you pray the joined prayers at 'Arafat.

When you arrive in Makka it is best to go to the Sacred Mosque as soon as possible and to enter it by the gate of Banu Shayba. Once inside the mosque, you should make for the Black Stone.

If you can kiss it or touch it you should do so, but if that is not possible owing to the throng of people around it you should at least gesture towards it, saying, "*Allahu akbar*" as you do so.

Then, starting from there, you join the endless wheel of the *tawaf*, revolving anti-clockwise around the Ancient House. In this the first *tawaf* of the *Hajj*, men should bare their right shoulders and the first three circuits of the Ka'ba should be done at a kind of half-running half-walking pace and the last four at a normal walk. You should make sure you go outside the semi-circular wall of the *Hijr Isma'il*, which is on the side of the Ka'ba opposite the Black Stone. Each time you pass the Black Stone you should kiss or touch it if that is possible (which is not always the case) or at any rate gesture towards it saying, "*Allahu akbar*" and you should also honour the Yamani Corner, which is the one before the Black Stone corner, but by touching it rather than kissing it.

Once you have completed your seven circuits you should go to the *Maqam Ibrahim*, which is the area opposite the side of the Ka'ba containing the door, and pray two *rak'ats* there. Then, having drunk some water from Zamzam, you make your way to the rock of Safa to begin your *sa'y*. You climb up on to the rock and stand there facing the Ka'ba for a time making supplication. From there you join the crowd of people walking the few hundred metres to Marwa. There is a stretch in the middle marking the old river bed which is indicated by two green markers, between which you should quicken your pace to a run. When you reach Marwa you climb up it and make supplication facing the Ka'ba as you did on Safa. Then you return to Safa, do the same there again and return to Marwa, going backwards and forwards between them until you have covered the distance seven times which will leave you at Marwa. With this the rite of *sa'y* is completed. If you are doing what is known as *Hajj at-tamattu'* you should now cut your hair and come out of *ihram* which you will re-enter when you leave Makka for Mina. If you are doing either of the two other types of *Hajj* you remain in *ihram*.

On the 8th day of Dhu'l-Hijja all those intending to do the *Hajj* leave Makka for the valley of Mina where they spend the night, praying there the prayers of *Dhuhr, 'Asr, Maghrib, 'Isha* and *Subh* the following morning, which is 9th Dhu'l-Hijja, after which everyone leaves for the plain of 'Arafat. Having arrived at 'Arafat you spend the rest of the day there in *dhikr* and supplication, joining the prayers of *Dhuhr* and *'Asr* at the beginning of the time of *Dhuhr,* and then immediately after sunset you leave 'Arafat for Muzdalifa without praying *Maghrib.* When you arrive at Muzdalifa, which is about midway between 'Arafat and Mina, you join the prayers of *Maghrib* and *'Isha.* You spend the night there in the open, remembering to gather forty-nine or seventy small stones (depending on whether you intend to stay two or three days in Mina) to stone the *jamarat* columns at Mina. After praying the *Subh* prayer of 10th Dhu'l-Hijja at Muzdalifa you make your way as quickly as you can back to Mina where your first duty is to throw seven of the stones you have collected at the *Jamra al-'Aqaba* column, calling out "*Allahu akbar*" as you cast each one.

Now is the time to sacrifice an animal if you are going to do that and following that men should shave their heads or cut some of their hair off, although the former is considered better, but women should only cut off a short length of hair. Following that you return to Makka to do the *Tawaf al-Ifada* and once you have completed that, you come out of *ihram* and all the things which were forbidden, such as grooming yourself, are permitted again. You then return to Mina where you spend either two or three days, depending on how much time you have available, and during them on each day you stone each of the *jamarat* in turn saying "*Allahu akbar*" with each stone as you did before, ending up with the *Jamra al-'Aqaba.*

When you have thrown your last stone and made supplication the rites of *Hajj* are completed. You return to Makka for the rest of your stay there and you should try and make the last thing you do before finally leaving your farewell *tawaf.* It is also strongly recommended that part of your time in the Hijaz, either before or after *Hajj*, should be spent in Madina visiting the Mosque of the Prophet ﷺ and other places mentioned in the books of *sira*.

Those who have performed *Hajj* coupled with *'umra* (*tamattu'* or *qiran*) must sacrifice an animal, or fast three days during the *Hajj* and seven when they return home.

THE SPIRITUAL BENEFITS OF *HAJJ*

"The *Hajj* is the demonstration of the reality that in Islam all roads lead to the House of Allah, where nationality, race, and difference of doctrine are all blown away. The *Hajjis* come from everywhere, from every country, every continent and every background. They come flying, sailing and by land. But whoever they are, wherever they come from and however they come, they are drawn by only one thing and to only one point – their desire to worship Allah at His House and perform the rites of the *Hajj*.

"From the moment he sets out with the intention of performing *Hajj*, the *Hajji's* journey is in one sense not his own – in that he is just one of millions of others doing exactly the same thing – and yet in another sense it is uniquely his own – since within that great gathering he will stand alone face to face with his Lord in the unfolding of his own unshared individual destiny. He becomes one of the many elements heading for the crucible of Makka where the great fusing of the Muslim community takes place, where all the parts are thrown together under the most intense conditions, mixed, melted together and then finally separated out again and returned to their homes never quite the same as when they left."

These are the words of a British Muslim written after he returned from *Hajj* in 1976 and although that is quite a few years ago now, *Hajj* is timeless in many ways and they are certainly as true today as they were then. Almost no one comes back from their *Hajj* unaltered. With some returning *Hajjis* the change is only superficial; the gloss disappears quickly; and within a very short time they are exactly as they were before. Others, however,

The Natural Form of Man

come back utterly transformed, their lives take on a new and more meaningful quality; they are those the Prophet ﷺ referred to as becoming as if they were newly born; for them the *Hajj* really has acted as a new beginning to their lives.

It is not sufficient just to participate passively in the rites of *Hajj*, just to get swept along with the flow like a piece of flotsam; you have to bring something to them from within yourself and that "something" is *taqwa*, fearful awareness of Allah. The rites are not magical, by which I mean that they have no automatically beneficial effect on those who perform them. Certainly there is great blessing in them stemming from the ancientness of their Divine prescription and from the billions of believers who have participated in them down through the centuries. But the benefit someone personally will derive from them is directly proportional to the amount of *taqwa* they bring to them.

Perhaps the most comprehensive statement ever made concerning this inward dimension of *Hajj* was made by Junayd al-Baghdadi, the great third-century scholar, judge and sufi.

> A man came to visit Junayd and Junayd asked him where he had come from. He replied that he had just returned from *Hajj*. Junayd said to him, "From the time you left your home did you also leave behind all wrong action?"
>
> "No," replied the man.
>
> "Then you never really left at all. At every stop you made on the way, did you also advance another stage on the path to Allah?"
>
> "No," came the reply.
>
> "Then you did not really make the journey. When you put on your *ihram* at the *miqat*, did you discard the attributes of selfhood as you took off your ordinary clothes?"
>
> "No," once more.
>
> "Then you did not really take on *ihram*. When you did *tawaf* of the Ka'ba, did you witness the beauty of Allah in the abode of purification?"

"No, I did not," said the man.

"Then you did not really do *tawaf*. When you did *sa'y* between Safa and Marwa did you reach the rank of *safa* (purity) and *muruwwa* (virtue)?" [a play on the two names Safa and Marwa]

"No." "Then you did not really do *sa'y*. When you went out to Mina did your *muna* (desires) cease?"

"No, they did not."

"Then you never really went to Mina. When you stood on 'Arafa did you experience even a single moment of *ma'rifa* (direct knowledge) of Allah?"

"No."

"Then you did not really stand on 'Arafa. When you stayed the night at Muzdalifa did you renounce your love of this world?"

"No, I did not."

"Then you did not really stay at Muzdalifa. When you stoned the *Jamra*, did you cast away from yourself everything that stands between you and your Lord."

"No."

"Then you did not really do the stoning. When you made your sacrifice, did you offer up your lower self to Allah?"

"Then you did not really make a sacrifice and the truth is that you have not properly performed *Hajj* at all. Return and do the *Hajj* again in the manner I have described so that you may finally truly attain to the *Maqam* of Ibrahim."

Now obviously if we take this literally I doubt that these days even one *Hajj* a year would be acceptable according to Imam Junayd's stringent criteria – but what his words do indicate very clearly is that there is an essential inner dimension to the *Hajj*. At the same time it is vital to point out that Imam Junayd's words do not involve any kind of inward/outward dichotomy, some kind of inward meaning to the *Hajj* separate from the outward form. They rather show that, as in all our acts of worship, every outward act of the *Hajj* has a corresponding and inseparable inner reality without which it cannot be considered complete, just as an egg without its white and yolk is no longer properly speaking an egg but merely an eggshell.

The necessary inward dimension to the act of going into *ihram* takes the form of that intention on which the very validity of a person's *Hajj* depends and which should be projected forward into all the rites they are expecting to fulfil so that the whole of their *Hajj* will be imbued with it. After *ihram* Imam Junayd asks about *tawaf*, the act of circling Allah's House which is another of the essential components of the journey.

When one enters the great wheel which night and day incessantly revolves around the Ka'ba it is all too easy to become distracted by the amazing sight it represents and the pushing and shoving which is the inevitable accompaniment of so many people moving round in a limited space and which becomes particularly vigorous in the vicinity of the Black Stone. For this reason it is extremely important to keep a watch on one's heart, and one way to do this is to choose a simple invocation and to repeat it continually, remembering to change it to the Qur'anic *du'a* recommended by the Prophet 🕌 between the Yamani corner and the Black Stone. The circle of the *tawaf* is perhaps the place on *Hajj* where one is most aware of being a citizen of the world. Every continent, race, and nation is represented and, extraordinarily, the specific characteristics of each is evident in the way they perform the rite.

On another level the act of *tawaf* can be seen as a reflection of our lives as a whole. If you look carefully at your life you will see that it is not so much an unbroken progression from beginning to end as a series of cycles which tend to bring you back and back again to the same point in a kind of repeating pattern. This pattern has its high point and low point, a little like a comet whose orbit comes close to the sun and then whizzes back off into deep space before returning once more to the light. This is mirrored in the *tawaf* by the passing of the Black Stone and the energy generated when that happens. What is to be desired both in our lives as a whole and in our *tawaf* is that our circling should not, as it were, remain always at the same level but should rather take the form of an upward spiral so that each time we pass the same point we have come that much closer to Allah than we were the previous time round.

The *tawaf* ends with two *rak'ats* at the *Maqam* of Ibrahim and this really is an exercise which has great meaning for our lives at large. Somehow, in the midst of all the hustle and bustle of the *Haram*, at the edge of, or even within the compass of, the endless wheeling of the *tawaf* crowd, we have to carve out a space for ourselves and locate a few moments of stillness and concentration in which we can stand, bow, prostrate and devote ourselves to the worship of our Lord.

One other definite spiritual benefit connected with the House of Allah has as much to do with people who are not there as those who are. The short length of wall between the door of the Ka'ba and the corner containing the Black Stone is known as *al-Multazam*. If you look at a picture of that side of the Ka'ba you will always see people spreadeagled against the wall at that point, almost as if they are trying to enter the House directly through the wall, and when you are there you will hear and feel the intensity of the supplication in that place and there is scarcely an eye there that will not be flooded with tears.

It is said that all supplications made there are answered and everyone at some time during their visit to the *Masjid al-Haram* should try to take advantage of the opportunity it offers to ask Allah's help and blessing, not just for themselves but also for those they left behind. There are, of course, endless chances during the *Hajj* in many of the holy places to make such supplications, and in this way something of the spiritual benefits of *Hajj* reach many people who are not there to profit from the experience in person.

After *tawaf* comes *sa'y* which in a way reminds one of the rush hour in one of the great cities of the world. An endless seething mass of people flooding ceaselessly backwards and forwards in a paradoxical integration of confusion and order. *Sa'y* is a reenactment of the desperate search for water by Hajar, the wife of the Prophet Ibrahim ﷺ when she and her young son 'Isma'il were placed by him in the Hands of Allah in the barren valley of Bakka. She ran backwards and forwards between the two rocks of Safa and Marwa, climbing first onto the one and then onto the other searching every horizon for that group of travellers who would save them from their plight or for any trace of water.

In the end, what they needed appeared literally under their feet with the emergence of the spring of Zamzam. How often we do the same thing in our own lives. We cast about here and there, desperately seeking help of one kind or another from this one or that one, usually forgetting that Allah, may He be exalted, is well aware of our circumstances, and then Allah's help arrives from right under our noses or sometimes even from within ourselves and the situation is resolved.

Like all the rites of *Hajj* the act of *sa'y* is packed with wisdom and many different insights can be gained from its performance. Shaykh Abdalqadir as-Sufi has this to say about it in his seminal work, *The Way of Muhammad*:

> When the *Hajji* begins his *sa'y*, he joins an already moving bank of people between the two rocks of Safa and Marwa, so that the stream of people between the two Waymarks is endless. As you fall into that sea of activity rushing from here to there and there to here, and the ocean of faces washes past you, some seen again and again, others seen once and for all, the rhythmic running from a place to a place takes on the impulse of activity that has governed all one's life of forgetfulness. All the struggle and fretfulness of existence, all the coming and going, becomes condensed into these seven terrible flights from A to B and from B to A. Seven times is enough for the life of one to be exposed to one's palpitating heart.

The next step on the *Hajj* is the move to Mina. It is perhaps at Mina that the reality of the *umma* of Islam is most clearly to be seen.

People tend to be camped according to the geographical area of the world from which they come so that at Mina all the races and nations of Islam more or less preserve their ethnic and national distinctions and yet are all in close juxtaposition to one another within a confined area. So for a few precious days communities normally separated by thousands of miles find themselves right next door to one another and in the benign atmosphere of *Hajj* that brotherhood of Islam, which is so elusive in today's artificially divided world, finds genuine and heartwarming expression, as Muslims from every part of the globe meet and enjoy the pleasure of one another's company. What is also made apparent is how much was lost by the Muslims with the breakup of the *khilafa* and how much the Muslims stand to gain from the political reunification of the *umma* once more under one *khalifa*.

The Prophet ﷺ said, "*Hajj* is 'Arafa," (Ahmad, Abu Dawud, at-Tirmidhi, Ibn Majah, an-Nasa'i) so it is evident that the great gathering of the *Hajjis* on the plain of 'Arafa is the core rite of *Hajj*. This is what everyone has come for. There is no doubt that in an almost explicit way it prefigures that Final Gathering which all human beings will inevitably attend on the Last Day. It is there at 'Arafa that the reality of the state of *ihram* is made most manifest. The lives of all who are present are stripped down to the barest essentials.

All distinctions are removed. Wealth and poverty, every kind of class distinction, all the things which normally set people apart from one another in their worldly lives, all these things are set aside and all that remains is the simple fact of their common humanity. All they have is their actions, what they have done with themselves up to that point, what they have turned themselves into by what they have done; nothing more and nothing less than what they truly are. It is a priceless opportunity to take stock. All stand there, as it were naked, in front of their Lord, with all the normal distractions and cushions taken away, face to face with Allah with nothing in between but the veil of their own existence.

There is nothing for anyone to do there but turn to Allah with complete sincerity and call on Him making their *deen* sincerely His, hoping for His forgiveness, longing for His mercy and yearning for the vision of His noble Face; and truly there is nowhere and no time on earth where people's prayers are more likely to find acceptance. Jabir reported Allah's Messenger ﷺ as saying:

> When they Day of 'Arafa comes, Allah descends to the lowest heaven and praises the people there to the angels, saying, "Look at My slaves who have come to Me dishevelled, dusty and crying out from every deep valley. I call you to witness that I have forgiven them." Then the angels object, saying, "But my Lord this man has done such and such a thing and also that woman…" Allah, Who is great and glorious replies, "I have forgiven them." (Ibn Abi'd-Dunya, al-Bazzar, Ibn Khuzayma, 'Abd ar-Razzaq, Sa'id ibn Mansur, Ibn 'Asakir)

Shaykh Abdalqadir says about 'Arafa in *The Way of Muhammad*:

> It is a rite that takes man back to his origin, for 'Arafa is the meeting point, the point of the reunion on earth of Adam and Hawwa (Eve). It is the source point of the human situation. The meaning of the *Hajj* and its reality lies in this 'moment', this time at the source of life itself, and what the *Hajji* does is stop. Stand on 'Arafa – it was for this that the journey was undertaken. Alone on a wide desert plain surrounded by a throng of others identical to yourself, bare-headed and draped in two white cloths – many there will be buried in these same cloths – you just come to a halt; quite simply, exhausted, dazed, you stop. At that moment there is absolutely nowhere to go. You are there. With Allah. The journey is accomplished. After that everything is purification and supplication.

The three rites of the *Eid al-Adha* at Mina are stoning the

Jamra al-'Aqaba, sacrificing an animal and shaving the head. All of them represent very specific actions and in one way the meaning of them is inextricably bound up with the actual doing of them and unfolds for every individual as they take place. But, of course, much has been written about them over the centuries and everyone inevitably reflects on their significance before and after actually performing them. Stoning the *jamras* is often referred to as stoning Shaytan. Allah warns us against Shaytan and informs us unequivocally that he is our enemy and perhaps one lesson we can learn is that even on this most blessed of days, the *Eid al-Adha,* people are not safe from Shaytan's insinuations and must protect themselves from them.

Shaykh Ibn 'Arabi al-Hatimi takes that one step further in his explanation of the rite. He says that at 'Arafa we purify our understanding of Allah's unity and rid ourselves of the tendency to associate other things with Him and that in throwing the seven stones on the *Eid* the next day we are casting out of ourselves certain Shaytan-inspired thoughts that make us associate other things with Allah and that is why we call out "*Allahu akbar*" as we throw – by declaring Allah to be greater, people are disassociating Him from their tendency to commit *shirk* which Shaytan has tried to instil into their thinking process. So rather than throwing stones at Shaytan we are casting out from ourselves shaytanic thoughts.

As is made plain in the *ayat* in *Surat al-Hajj* which refers to it (22:35), Allah, blessed is He and exalted, is Himself concerned that people understand that the important element in the rite of sacrifice is that awareness of Him (*taqwa*) in them which must accompany the physical act and which alone imbues it with meaning. We should remember that it commemorates the occasion when Ibrahim ﷺ was absolved from having to sacrifice his beloved son and given a ram to sacrifice in his stead. So what the rite indicates is our preparedness to give up what is most precious to us for the sake of Allah.

The thing more precious to us than anything else is our own

selfhood, our own independent existence, and so, in its highest sense, the sacrifice represents our willingness to give up our own will and submit ourselves entirely to the will of our Lord; and the truth is that by doing this we stand to lose nothing and to gain our heart's desire. Allah, exalted is He, says in *Surat at-Tawba*: "*Allah has bought from the believers their selves and their wealth in return for the Garden,*" and then at the end of the *ayat*: "*Rejoice then in the bargain you have made. That is the great victory.*" (9:112)

The sheer physical relief of removing the accumulated dust and grime and dishevelment of our days in *ihram* in itself gives a more than adequate meaning to the act of shaving the head and the cleaning process which accompanies it. It really does give one a sense of starting life all over again. It is this very feeling which validates a slightly more symbolic interpretation of the rite which is, that in getting rid of your hair you are in a certain sense stripping away your past and that the new hair growth as it emerges truly is indicative of a new beginning to your life as a whole.

One important aspect of the journey to the Hijaz is the visit to Madina al-Munawwara. This is strongly recommended to the point of being considered a *sunna* of the *Hajj* journey. Qadi 'Iyad said about it, "Visiting the tomb of the Prophet ﷺ is a *sunna* among the Muslims on which there is unanimous agreement. It is a virtue which is encouraged." If Makka is a crucible where the *Hajji* is purged and purified, Madina is a pool of tranquillity where he finds peace and refreshment. Remember that it was in Madina that the social reality of Islam was first given form, where the justice and compassion of Islam found their most perfect expression, that city about whose inhabitants Allah Himself said, "*You are the best community ever to be produced before mankind.*" (3:110)

What was latent and implicit during the Prophet's ﷺ long and difficult years in Makka, became realised and explicit in Madina and a community of human beings, living according to the laws of Allah by following the example of His Messenger ﷺ, brought about the best human social situation ever to have existed on the surface of the earth. It is the resonance of this which emanates from the grave of the Prophet ﷺ and still pervades the city which welcomed him and made it possible for Islam to be implemented in its totality.

One does not have to go too far to discover the spiritual benefits of the visit to Madina. What blessing could be greater than being greeted by the Messenger of Allah himself ﷺ and, as he himself said, that is what happens to all who greet him in his grave. In the famous hadith from Abu Hurayra ﷺ related by Ahmad, Abu Dawud and al-Bayhaqi, he said ﷺ "There is no one who greets me but that Allah will return my spirit to me so that I can return the greeting to him." And certainly there are very few *Hajjis* who do not experience something of the sweetness of the Prophetic presence during their stay in Madina. So just as the *Hajj* itself imbues one with a greater sense of the Divine presence and fosters love of Allah in the heart, the visit to Madina opens the heart to greater love for His Messenger ﷺ and by extension to love for the whole *umma* of Islam.

The point of mentioning these things has been to indicate something of the inner dimension of the various rites of *Hajj*. But in the end, although such indications may perhaps open a door or two to a deeper appreciation of the *Hajj*, it is only a person's own tasting of the acts themselves which will really be of any use to them. It is only your direct experience of the rites of *Hajj* which will actually constitute your *Hajj*, and your *Hajj* will inevitably be uniquely your own, totally different from everyone else's, even that of someone who may have been alongside you for most of the time you were there. This is because the *Hajj* is as much an inward journey as an outward one and, as we have seen, it is that inward dimension, the unknowable amount of that outwardly indefinable but indispensable quality of *taqwa* which you bring to all the rites you perform, it is that and that alone on which the amount of benefit you receive from the *Hajj* and its acceptability to Allah in the end depends.

It is appropriate to finish with the *ayats* with which Allah concludes the *sura* which He dedicated to the institution of *Hajj*:

> *You who believe! bow and prostrate*
>> *and worship your Lord,*
>> *and do good, so that hopefully you will be successful.*
> *Do jihad for Allah with the jihad due to Him.*
>> *He has selected you and not placed*
>>> *any constraint upon you in the deen*
>> *the religion of your forefather Ibrahim.*
> *He named you Muslims before and also in this,*
>> *so that the Messenger could be witness against you*
>>> *and you could be witnesses against all mankind.*
>> *So establish salat and pay zakat*
>>> *and hold fast to Allah.*
>> *He is your Protector*
> *the Best Protector, the Best Helper.* (22:75-76)

IMAN

is to believe in Allah, His
angels, His Books, His
Messengers, and the Last Day,
and to believe in the Decree,
both its good and its evil.

Allah

The instruction to believe in Allah pervades the Qur'an and one third of the Qur'an is devoted to teaching human beings about the nature of the Divine Unity. It is said that all that teaching is summed up in *Surat al-Ikhlas*.

In the name of Allah, All-Merciful, Most Merciful
Say: He is Allah, Absolute Oneness.
Allah the Everlasting Sustainer of all.
He has not given birth and was not born.
And no one is comparable to Him. (112:1-4)

Two other representative passages dealing with the nature of the Divine Unity, are the well-known *Ayat al-Kursi* from *Surat al-Baqara*:

Allah,
there is no god but Him,
the Living, the Self-Sustaining.
He is not subject to drowsiness or sleep.
Everything in the heavens and the earth belongs to Him.
Who can intercede with Him except by His permission?
He knows what is before them and what is behind them
but they cannot grasp any of His knowledge
save what He wills.

His Footstool encompasses the heavens and the earth
and their preservation does not tire Him.
He is the Most High, the Magnificent. (2:253-4)

and the beginning of *Surat al-Hadid*:

Everything in the heavens and the earth glorifies Allah.
He is the Almighty, the All-Wise.
The kingdom of the heavens and the earth belongs to Him.
He gives life and causes to die.
He has power over all things.
He is the First and the Last, the Outward and the Inward.
He has knowledge of all things.
It is He Who created the heavens and the earth in six days,
then established Himself firmly on the Throne.
He knows what goes into the earth
and what comes out of it,
what comes down from heaven
and what goes up into it.
He is with you wherever you are – Allah sees what you do.
The kingdom of the heavens and the earth belongs to Him.
All things return to Allah.
He makes night merge into day and day merge into night.
He knows what the heart contains. (57:1-4)

Belief in Allah is the core of Islam and indeed essential to
the basic purpose of human life. Many non-Muslims claim to
believe in God but very few of them are able to come up with a
coherent definition of the deity they believe in. Knowledge of
what it is possible to say about the nature of the Divine Unity has
always been an essential element of Islamic teaching and, from
the very beginning, understanding of what can and cannot be
said about Allah has been obligatory for every Muslim. The
Qur'anic sources formed the basis of all the formulations of the
Divine unity expressed by scholars in the early days of Islam. An
example of this can be found in the *Risala* of Ibn Abi Zayd al-
Qayrawani. He wrote:

These obligatory tenets include believing in the heart and expressing with the tongue that Allah is One God with no god other than Him, nor any likeness to Him, nor any equal to Him. He has had no child. He had no father. He has no wife. He has no partner. There is no beginning to His firstness nor any end to His lastness.

Those who try to describe Him can never adequately do so nor can thinkers encompass Him in their thought. Real thinkers derive lessons from His signs but do not try to think about the nature of His Essence. *"But they do not attain any of His knowledge except what He wills."* (2:254) *"His Footstool embraces the heavens and the earth, and their preservation does not tire Him. He is the Most High, the Magnificent."* (2:254)

He is the All-Knowing and the All-Aware, the Arranger and the All-Powerful. The All-Hearing and the All-Seeing. The High and the Great. He is over His Glorious Throne by His Essence. He is everywhere by His knowledge. *"He created man and He knows what his self whispers to him and He is nearer to him than his jugular vein."* (50:16) *"No leaf falls without Him knowing of it nor is there any seed in the darkness of the earth, nor any fresh thing nor any dry thing, that is not in a clear book."* (6:60) He is established on His throne and has absolute control over His kingdom.

He has the most beautiful names and the most sublime attributes and He has always had all these names and attributes. He is exalted above any of His attributes ever having been created or any of His names having been brought into temporal existence.

He spoke to Musa (Moses) with His speech which is an attribute of His essence and not something created. He manifested Himself to the mountain and it disintegrated through exposure to His majesty.

This understanding is based entirely on the way the first

generations of Islam understood those verses of the Qur'an which refer directly to the Divine Unity. Quite soon, however, various factions of rationalists and literalists began to distort this straightforward acceptance of the revealed text and it became necessary to structuralise the understanding of the Divine Attributes to defend this orthodox belief. One of the great scholars who took on the defence of the original Qur'anic understanding was Imam Abu'l-Hasan al-Ash'ari.

Basing himself firmly on the original Qur'anic understanding, he organised the understanding of the Divine Attributes in a such a way that the danger of people making a mistake about the nature of the God they worshipped was reduced to an absolute minimum. He elicited thirteen essential attributes, six of which applied to the Divine Essence and seven to the Divine actions. Those describing the Divine Essence are:

1. Existence/*wujud*. Properly speaking, existence/*wujud* is not an attribute as such, but denotes simply the fact that Allah *is*.
2. Pre-eternity/*qidam*
3. Going on forever/*baqa*
4. Absolute lack of need/*ghina*
5. Differentiation from created beings/*mukhalafa li'l-hawadith*
6. Unity of His essence, attributes and actions/*wahdaniyya dhatihi wa sifatihi wa af'alihi*

The Divine attributes necessary for Divine action are:

7. Life/*hayat*
8. Knowledge/*'ilm*
9. Power/*qudra*
10. Will/*irada*
11. Hearing/*sam'a*
12. Sight/*basar*
13. and Speech/*kalam*

The Natural Form of Man

Basing themselves on the Qur'an in the context of this concise framework, scores of scholars have, over the centuries, expanded on them and given comprehensive descriptions of the Divine Unity. Among them is that of Abu Bakr al-Kalabadhi:

Allah is One, Alone, Single, Eternal, Everlasting, Knowing, Powerful, Living, Hearing, Seeing, Strong, Mighty, Majestic, Great, Generous, Clement, Proud, Awesome, Enduring, Lord, Sovereign, Master, Merciful, Compassionate, Willing, Speaking, Creating and Sustaining. He is qualified with all the attributes with which He has qualified Himself and named with all the names with which He has named Himself. From pre-eternity He has never ceased to continue with all these names and attributes without resembling creation in any way. His Essence does not resemble the essence of any created thing nor His Attributes their attributes. No term applied to created beings, and indicating their creation in time, has currency over Him. He has not ceased to be the First, the Foremost before all things born in time, the Existent before everything. There is nothing eternal except Him and no deity besides Him. He is not a body or shape or form or person or element or accident. With Him there is no joining or separation, no movement or rest, no increase or decrease. He has no parts or particles or members or limbs or aspects or places. He has no faults, is never overcome by sleep, is not affected by states and cannot be defined by allusions. He is not contained by space or affected by time. He cannot be said to be touched or isolated or to dwell in any place. He cannot be encompassed by thought or covered by a veil or perceived by the eye. His attributes do not change and His names do not alter. This has never ceased to be the case and never will cease to be the case. He is the First, the Last, the Outward and the Inward. He knows all things. There is nothing like Him. And He sees and hears all things.

'Ali al-Hujwiri says on the same theme:

Allah is One, incapable of union and separation, not admitting duality. His Unity is not numerical such that it would be made two by the addition of another number. He is not finite so as to have the six directions. He has no space and is not in space so as to require the predication of space. He is not contingent so as to need a substance, nor a substance which cannot exist without another like itself. He is not a natural form which would make Him subject to motion and rest. He is not a spirit so as to need a frame. He is not a physical body so as to be composed of limbs. He does not become imminent in things which would mean they were in some way homogenous with Him. He is not joined to anything because that would mean that that thing was part of Him. He is free from all imperfections and exalted above all defects. He has no like so that He and His creature should make two. He has no child whose birth would necessarily make him a sire. His essence and attributes are unchangeable. He is endowed with those attributes of perfection which the believers and those who affirm His unity confirm and which He has described Himself as possessing. He is free of those attributes which heretics impute to Him. He is the Living, Knowing, Forgiving, Merciful, Willing, Powerful, Hearing, Seeing, Speaking, and Subsistent. His knowledge is not produced in Him nor is His power induced in Him. His hearing and sight are not separable from Him. His speech is not apart from Him. He has existed together with His attributes from pre-eternity. No created thing is outside His knowledge or independent of His will. He does whatever He wills and wills whatever He sees fit and no creature can gainsay Him in that. His decree is final, so His friends have no recourse except resignation to it. He is the Sole Predestinator of good and evil and the only true source of hope and fear. He creates all benefit and harm. He alone gives judgement and His judgement is wisdom. No one can reach Him. The inhabitants of the Garden will see Him. Anthropomorphism does not apply to him so that anyone could be face to face with Him or see Him with their eyes. However, the friends of Allah may contemplate Him in this world.

Muhyi'd-Din ibn 'Arabi expanded even further on this basic picture:

My brothers and loved ones, may Allah be pleased with you! A weak, poor slave in need of Allah in every phrase and glance calls on you to testify for him after calling on Allah, His angels and whoever is present of the believers and hears, to testify that he testifies in word and belief that:

Allah is one without second in His divinity, free of any spouse or child, the Master without partner, the King without any minister.

He is the Doer without any manager alongside Him.

He exists by Himself without need of anyone to bring Him into existence. Indeed, everything else in existence is in need of Him for its existence. The entire universe exists by Him and He alone is described as having existence by Himself.

There is no beginning to His existence and no end to His going-on. It is pure, unlimited existence.

He is Self-subsistent, not based on an isolated substance (*jawhar*) which would determine a place for Him, nor anything contingent (*'arad*) which would make it impossible for Him to go on, nor on a body which would possess a direction and have an opposite.

He is pure above having any directions and regions.

He can be seen by the hearts and eyes if He so wishes.

He "*settled himself on His Throne*", as He said (7:54), and that is according to the meaning He meant, as is also the case with the Throne and whatever else He settles on. He is the First and Last.

He has no intelligible semblance and intellects cannot indicate Him. Time does not limit Him nor place lessen Him. He *was* without place, and He *is* now in the state that He was.

He created that which is firmly established as well as place, and he originated time. He said, "I am the One, the Living Who is not tired by sustaining creatures." No attribute which He did not have in formation of things can refer to Him.

He is exalted above in-time events residing in Him, or Him in them, or being before or after Him. It is said, "He was, and nothing was with Him." "Before" and "after" are part of the restrictions of time which He originated.

He is the Self-Subsistent (*Qayyum*) Who does not sleep, the Conqueror Who does not budge. *"Nothing is like Him."* (42:11)

He created the Throne and made it the limit of settling. He originated the Footstool which encompasses the heavens and the earth.

He is the High Who originated the Tablet and Pen and made it write a Book by His knowledge about His creation until the Day of Separation and Decision.

He originated the entire universe without prior example. He created creation. How excellent is His creation!

He sent down the spirits (*arwah*) into forms as trustees and made these forms, into which He sent the spirits, viceregents on earth.

He subjected to us all that is in the heavens and the earth. Not an atom moves but to Him and from Him.

He created everything without any need of it or anything obliging Him to do that, but His knowledge preceded His creation of what He created.

"He is the First and the Last, the Outward and the Inward." (57:3) *"He has power over all things."* (11:4) *"He encompasses all things in His knowledge."* (65:12) *"He has counted the exact*

number of everything." (72:28) "*He knows your secrets and what is even more concealed.*" (20:7) "*He knows the eyes' deceit and what people's breasts conceal.*" (40:19) How can He not know a thing when He created it? "*Does He Who created not then know? He is the All-Pervading, the All-Aware.*" (67:14)

He knew things before they existed and then brought them into existence according to a limit only He knows. He still knows things and His knowledge is not renewed when things are renewed. Through His knowledge He perfected things and by His knowledge He makes whomever He wills rule them. He knows universals absolutely as He knows specific matters, by the consensus and agreement of the people of sound investigation. He is "*the Knower of the Unseen and Visible,*" (13:10) "*Allah is far above what they associate with Him.*" (7:189)

"*Doing what He will*" (11:108), He transforms things in the world of the earth and the heavens. His power is not connected to anything until He wills it and He does not will it until He knows it since it is logically impossible that He would will something that He did not know.

So in existence there is no obedience or disobedience, profit or loss, slave or free, cold or hot, life or death, attainment or relinquishment, day or night, balance or bias, land or sea, even or odd, substance or accident, health or illness, joy or sorrow, spirit or form, darkness or light, earth or heaven, composition or decomposition, many or few, branch or root, white or black, sleep or wakefulness, outward or inward, moving or still, dry or wet, surface or core, or any of these opposite relations, differences and correspondences except that it is willed by Allah the Great.

How can it not be what He willed when He brought it into existence? How can what is chosen exist if it were not willed? There is no averting His command and no revising His judgement.

"*He gives sovereignty to whomever He wills and takes sovereignty away from whomever He wills. He exalts whoever He wills and abases whomever He wills."* (3:26) *"He misguides whomever He wills and guides whomever He wills."* (35:8) Whatever He wills to be, *is*. Whatever He does not will to be, *is not*.

If all creatures were to band together to will something which Allah did not will that they will, they would not have willed or done anything that Allah did not will should be brought into existence. They will it when He wills that they will it and otherwise they would not do it nor are they able to do it nor have they the power to do it.

Disbelief and belief, obedience and disobedience are all by His will, wisdom and volition. He is described with this will from before-time.

The universe was non-existent, not in existence, even though it was fixed in its source in knowledge. Then He brought the universe into existence without reflection or thought. There was no ignorance or lack of knowledge so that reflection and thought would give Him knowledge of what He did not know. He is too majestic and exalted for that! Rather, He brought the universe into existence from prior knowledge and the determination of the pure pre-eternal will which demanded what the universe contains in terms of time and space, beings and colours, with which He brought it into existence. In reality, there is nothing in existence which possesses will except Him, since He – glory be to Him! – says, *"You only will what Allah wills."* (76:30; 81:29)

As He knows, so He determines. He wills and so apportions. He decrees and brings into existence. He hears and sees whatever moves or is still or speaks in mankind, from the lowest and highest worlds. Distance does not veil His hearing for He is Near. Nearness does not veil His sight for He is Far. He hears the self speaking to itself and the sound of the lightest touch. He sees blackness in the darkness and water in the water. Neither mixture nor darkness nor light veils Him. *"He is All-Hearing, All-Seeing."*

The Natural Form of Man

He speaks, but not from prior silence or imaginary stillness, but with pre-eternal timeless speech – just as is the case with all His attributes – knowledge, will and power. He spoke to Musa, peace be upon him. He called it *"Revelation"*, the *Zabur* (Psalms), the *Torah* and the *Injil*. It is without letters, voices, notes or languages. He is the Creator of voices, letters and languages.

His speech is without uvula or language as His hearing is without auditory meatus or ears, as His sight is without eye or eye-lid, His will exists without being in a heart, His knowledge is without exigency or investigation of proof, and His life is without the energy from the inside of the heart which arises from the mixture of elements. So His Essence does not admit of increase or decrease.

Glory be to Him! Glory be to Him! Near to the far, Immense in power, with all-embracing charity and vast in favour. All that is other-than-Him flows from His generosity, favour and justice. He expands and contracts.

He perfected the making of the universe which He originated when He brought it into existence. He has no partner in His domain and no manager in His kingdom.

Glory be to Him! There is no doer except Him! There is nothing that exists for itself from itself except Him. *"Allah created both you and what you do."* (37:96) *"He will not be questioned about what He does, but they will be questioned."* (21:23) *"Allah's is the conclusive argument. If He had willed, He could have guided every one of you."* (6:149)

What must be borne in mind when reading these descriptions of the Divine Unity is that they are not in any way intellectual abstractions but, on the contrary, describe a most immediate reality and have an urgent significance and direct relevance to the life of every human being. What they are saying and what Allah Himself makes abundantly clear, time and time again in the Qur'an, is that nothing in existence has any power whatsoever except for Allah. *La hawla wala quwwata illa billah –*

There is no power or strength except with Allah. *La fa'il fi'l wujud siwa'llah* – There is no active agent in existence apart from Allah. This is the truth and it means that everything which happens, happens by Allah alone. The problem for us is that all of us, from a very early age, have had precisely the opposite drilled into us, that in the so-called real world Allah has nothing to do with what goes on and that, in fact, it is secondary causes which really make things happen. Do not underestimate how deeply the scientific materialist world view has penetrated into human consciousness, Muslim and non-Muslim. It is a thorough and continual indoctrination process with which we are being bombarded every day of our lives.

According to the prevalent worldview, wind and rain are brought about by pressure changes in the atmosphere and the rain cycle; the cause of plant growth is the nitrogen cycle; flight occurs through the science of aerodynamics; our own birth is solely the result of the human conception and gestation process; illnesses are cured by the science of medicine; the examples are endless. But it is simply not true. It is not that these things do not take place. They do. But they are not the reason for anything; they are not the cause of anything. Both cause and effect are directly created by Allah. Nothing makes anything happen except Allah.

In the Qur'an the whole matter is made crystal clear. It is Allah Who brings about the rainfall and makes the plants grow: "*It is He who sends down water from the sky from which We bring forth growth of every kind.*" (6:100) Flight is by Allah alone: "*Have they not looked at the birds above them, with wings outspread and folded back? Nothing holds them up but the All-Merciful.*" (67:19) Allah is responsible for bringing us into the world: "*It is He who created you from earth, then from a drop of sperm, then from a clot of blood, then He brings you out as infants.*" (40:67) And Allah, exalted is He, is the Curer of illness: "*And when I am ill, it is He who heals me.*" (26:80)

Believers may say, 'Oh yes, of course!' to these words but if they look into their heart to see what they in fact believe about how things come about, very few really see the Hand of Allah in what happens. Do they really see them as coming from Allah or does their conditioning get in the way so that they in fact ascribe them to the process by which they happen. We live in this world of secondary causes so it is natural for us to see existence in those terms. The difference between us and our forebears is that they were taught the truth, it was their bedrock, and it was, therefore, much easier for them to cut through appearances and see things as they really are. We, on the other hand, have been indoctrinated in a lie to the extent that it has become almost impossible for us to see things as they really are.

One significant way in which knowledge of Allah directly impinges on our day-to-day lives is in the matter of *rizq* – provision. Allah, blessed is He and exalted, is *ar-Razzaq* – the Provider. He alone continually nourishes and sustains everything in existence – including us. This means that the energy we expend to gain a livelihood, whatever form that may take, is not in reality the cause of our getting what we need. It is Allah Who provides for us. It is vital for people to understand the implications of this.

The culture we live in – and it is now clear that there is a single economic system which covers every part of the globe – is completely governed by the economic imperative. As we know, this present system is certainly more wide-spread and dominant than at any previous time in the whole of human history. It has gained its hold by the unscrupulous use of usurious financial techniques which have now enmeshed the whole world in a web of banks, markets and financial institutions, in which both nations and individuals are trapped in a spiral of unpayable debt. As a direct consequence of this, human life everywhere in the world is now basically defined in economic terms and human aspiration in terms of economic goals.

Children are taught at school that their career, their future employment, is the only thing in their life that really matters and their whole education is geared towards that end. And the result is that anxiety about employment or lack of it, about income or lack of it, is what in fact occupies most people's hearts and minds and what forms the subject matter of much of their conversation. And the whole way this global order has been able to hold everyone – Muslims as well as non-Muslims – in its thrall is by convincing them that their livelihood is entirely dependent on the system as it is set up. It is only the sword of *tawhid* – true knowledge of the Divine Unity – which can slice through the smothering web and set people free. People must remember that their livelihood is dependent on Allah alone and on nothing else whatsoever so what should concern them most is their awareness of and obedience to Allah, their Lord and Creator.

The glory of *tawhid* is not simply that it is a wondrous intellectual science, which it undoubtedly is, but that it has been a lived reality for generations of Muslims in all corners of the earth, as we know it will be for future generations. It is for our generation to reclaim it in an authentic fashion.

The Angels

...to believe in the angels

There are over a hundred references to angels and angelic activity in the Qur'an. A general mention is to be found at the beginning of *Surat al-Fatir*:

Praise be to Allah,
the Bringer into being of the heavens and the earth,
He who made the angels messengers,
with wings – two, three or four. (35:1)

The classical definition of the angels is that they are beings for whom wrong action is impossible. They do not disobey Allah in anything He commands and they carry out everything they are commanded to do. They are made of light and are neither male nor female. They do not eat or drink. This description is perfectly satisfactory for people for whom the existence of angels is a given, an accepted element in their world view. But many people of this time certainly do not have an automatic acceptance of angels and need a much more in-depth examination of the whole subject.

It is not devoutness to turn your faces
to the East or to the West.
Rather, those with true devotion are those who

believe in Allah and the Last Day,
* the Angels, the Book and the Prophets,*
and who, despite their love for it, give away their wealth
* to their relatives and to orphans and the very poor,*
and to travellers and beggars and to set slaves free,
* and who establish the prayer and pay zakat;*
those who honour their contracts when they make them,
* and are steadfast in poverty*
*   and in illness and in battle.*
Those are the people who are true.
* They are the godfearing. (2:177)*

This passage from the Qur'an, which includes a clear reference to the angels, outlines the underlying premises on which all the great traditional knowledge-systems of mankind have always been based. Behind all of them is the acceptance that we live in a universe created by One Divine Power surrounded by many unseen dimensions or angelic realms; that our existence on this earth is a short-lived affair whose significance lies in the fact that it is the realm of action whose result will become apparent in a further dimension of reality we will encounter when we die; and that Divine Guidance has come to tell us about all these things and to teach us how to live our lives in accordance with them. This, in brief, was the basic view of existence held by almost every human community from the beginning of human history down to the present age.

It is quite clear that up to a certain point in our history these basic realities remained unquestioned givens. In the European context the traditional view was, for instance, clearly expounded in the thirteenth century by Thomas Aquinas. According to Aquinas, all things proceed from God; and God is not only the ground of their being but also the supreme Good with which all seek to be reunited. God created the world in order that He might know Himself more completely. God not only created but continuously sustains the world and governs it both directly by the eternal laws and indirectly through angelic forces. To all creatures He has given a "nature" or "form" in virtue of which they are necessitated both to be what they are, and to seek that which is proper for them. Man is different from other creatures in that only he can aspire to know the Divine and in this lies his only fulfilment but he can either choose or deny this glorious possibility. Man is by his very nature oriented towards the supernatural world; he was created for knowledge of the Divine. This was basically how everyone understood the world they lived in and their place in it.

In Shakespeare's *Merchant of Venice* there is a speech addressed by Lorenzo to Jessica near the end of the play in which he says:

> There's not the smallest orb which thou behold'st
> But in this motion like an angel sings
> Still quiring to the young-eyed cherubins;
> Such harmony is in immortal souls;
> But, whilst this muddy vesture of decay
> Doth grossly close it in we cannot hear it.

So it is clear that in Shakespeare's time the traditional world-view was still firmly in place. The angelic world and the immortality of the human soul were still very much part and parcel of people's ordinary consciousness. Although Shakespeare's world was still sustained and nurtured by the old certainties, a new wind was blowing up which was shortly to reach gale force and wreak havoc with the traditional view leaving a very barren landscape in its place. Certainly John Donne, writing very few years later, is very explicit on the subject:

> And new philosophy calls all in doubt,
> The element of fire is quite put out;
> The sun is lost, and the earth, and no man's wit
> Can well direct him where to look for it.
> 'Tis all in pieces, all coherence gone;
> All just supply and all relation.

In the "new philosophy" the spiritual gave way to the material.

Men became concerned with quantity rather than quality. Human consciousness became more and more confined within the limits of the material universe. Basil Willey's seminal text, *The Seventeenth Century Background*, clearly and eloquently shows how the "new philosophy", scientific materialism in its germinal stages, penetrated and permeated the general consciousness. The pervasive nature of the scientific world view had a profound and far reaching effect on human consciousness. In fact for the human being the result was devastating. It was as if an impenetrable barrier became erected between the spiritual and material worlds and as the scientific world view inexorably imposed itself on and pervaded human consciousness, human beings became, in real terms, cut off from a true view of existence.

Up until this time people had been living at the centre of the universe with the sun and moon and stars revolving around them, above which were the celestial spheres of angelic activity all encompassed by the Throne of Allah, Whose unseen Hand moved and directed the whole affair. From now on people lived on an insignificant mineral mass, a mere part of a minor planetary system, one of countless others lost in the unimaginable vastness of limitless space. For the ordinary person it was just like being suddenly uprooted from a small village where everyone is known to each other, the hierarchy clear and unquestioned, all the relationships tried, tested and trusted, the atmosphere benign, all the paths well-trodden, every corner familiar, every livelihood assured, and off-loaded into the alienation and impersonality of a giant modern megalopolis whose barren streets seem to go on forever, where every quarter is the same yet unfamiliar, where the dominant energy is fear and mistrust, where even near neighbours are strangers.

Belief in God, which had been an inextricable part, a given, of the human situation, became at best an optional extra and increasingly frequently not an option at all. And, of course, as this happened, belief in the other foundational realities, the angelic worlds and Divine Revelation and human accountability, all of which, of course, depend on belief in God, were themselves eroded and all but washed away. How beautifully though despairingly Matthew Arnold expresses what happened in those famous lines of his poem *Dover Beach*:

> The Sea of Faith
> Was once, too, at the full, and round earth's shore
> Lay like the folds of a bright girdle furl'd.
> But now I only hear
> Its melancholy, long, withdrawing roar,
> Retreating to the breath
> Of the night wind, down the vast edges drear
> And naked shingles of the world.

And the tide has gone a long way further out since then.

The fact is that the inner fabric of Christendom, having been severely frayed by the storms of the Reformation was then completely ripped apart by the onslaught of the "new philosophy". This does not mean individual Christian beliefs or personal piety. What is being referred to is the legal and moral structure of European society. Christianity progressively lost its ability to impinge in any real way on society as a whole so that it is now obvious in so many ways that in social terms Christianity has disintegrated beyond the possibility of restoration and that it is demonstrably no longer capable of furnishing that clear guidance which is so necessary for there to be a healthy and just human situation.

Of all the traditional systems only Islam has survived complete and intact into our own time, still able to provide, unadulterated, a true picture of existence in all its vastness and splendour and the necessary guidance to bring about the social renewal which is so clearly vital at this time.

☆ ☆ ☆

In order to understand what angels are and the role they play in existence it is first essential to have some understanding of how existence functions, of the way creation unfolds, of the way the world we live in comes into being. It is clearly beyond the scope of this discussion to give an account of the whole creational process, and this is in no way intended to be that, but it is necessary to have the basic picture. Simply put there are three domains of existence known in Arabic as *Mulk, Malakut,* and *Jabarut.*

The last of these, *Jabarut,* is the domain of undifferentiated Divine Power, that indivisible Oneness which is at once the Fountainhead and Sustainer of all being and yet totally independent of it. The first of them, *Mulk,* is the domain of this world, the so-called material universe into which we emerge at birth and where we remain until we die, the space-time world of the seemingly solid objects of our day-to-day experience. The third term, *Malakut,* is the bridge between the two: The domain of Allah's Throne; the domain of the Mighty Pen and the Guarded Tablet whereby and on which all created things are written down, all that has happened up to now and all that will ever be; the domain of the Day of Judgement and all that happens on it; the domain of the Delights of Paradise and the Terrors of Hellfire; the domain of the eighteen thousand Unseen Worlds which have never been explored. And most importantly in the present context, the domain of the Angels, where they live and move and have their being.

All of this and everything that happens in existence takes place continually and instantly by direct Divine command. The angels are the means whereby these commands are carried out and this is where the overall function of the angelic forces in existence lies. An example that is sometimes used to help explain the angelic role in the creation as a whole is the way the body works. Think about what happens when you decide to get up from your seat. First of all an act of will is necessary, a decision to move, a central command. And then automatically, as if by magic, literally hundreds of coordinated separate movements and adjustments and readjustments occur spontaneously and you find yourself on your feet. The body moves as a harmonious whole but the process by which this takes place requires the transmission of hundreds of discrete electrical impulses conveying the instruction to stand up to every one of the different limbs, muscles and faculties concerned, simultaneously, unresistingly obedient to the command to move. As the electrical impulses are to the body, so are the angels to existence as a whole.

I would add at this point as a kind of caution that the angels and many of the things I have just been talking about belong outside the space-time continuum of our ordinary experience and perception and are therefore, properly speaking, beyond the scope of normal language to describe. The Prophet ﷺ once described the Garden as containing: "What the eye has not seen and the ear has not heard and the heart of man cannot conceive," (Al-Bukhari, Muslim) and this description can as well serve for the other matters of the Unseen. But we have no other access to knowing about these things except through human language, and Allah in the Qur'an and the Prophet ﷺ in his own statements use human language to tell us about realities which exist beyond space-time in the way that best indicates what they truly are.

We must, however, be careful on two counts. We must not imprison the descriptions within our own experience of material existence by taking them too literally but at the same time we must be careful not to etherialise them completely, and must realise that, when we meet them, the things involved will be recognisable from the description we were given. It is a little like reading a map. You have a clear idea about what you will find when you arrive but the reality is, of course, very different from the lines and symbols on the map. In the case of the angels our understanding of their nature and role is greatly amplified by what is in the Qur'an and in tradition so that we end up with a clear picture of angels and the angelic worlds they inhabit.

It should be said here that this could not be nor is it intended to be a complete and exhaustive description of the angelic realm. There are undoubtedly hierarchies upon hierarchies of innumerable angelic beings in existence whose splendour and magnificence are truly only known to Him Who brought them into being. One of the great blessings of Islam as man's final guidance is that we are only told of things on a need-to-know basis. We have been given neither more nor less than the knowledge we need to allow us to successfully navigate the shoals and turbulences of this life and ensure our safe arrival in the Next. Therefore although there are knowledges without number and rare beings who plumb the depths of some of them, the basic guidance of the Qur'an and the prophetic tradition contain all that is necessary for all human beings until the end of time. With regard to the angels we are told firstly of the four great angels who bestride, as it were, the angelic firmament in respect of mankind: Jibril, Mika'il, Azra'il and Israfil.

Of all the individual angels we know more about Jibril than any other and this is because of the specific function which he performs. Jibril is the angel of revelation. In a general sense this means that he is charged by Allah with informing mankind about the Divine Reality. Were it not for Jibril we would know nothing about Allah or His Laws or the purpose and possibilities of human existence on the earth. He is the means to all knowledge and awareness of Allah, Allah's messenger from Himself to human beings. Specifically, this, of course, meant that Jibril had an intimate connection with the Prophet Muhammad ﷺ during his life. He transmitted to him the words of Allah in the form of the Qur'an, visiting him regularly with different portions of the Revelation as they were needed over a period of more than twenty years. Jibril also acted as teacher and guide for the Prophet ﷺ on many other occasions throughout his life. One particular event to which we have already referred is the Night Journey and Ascension of the Prophet ﷺ when Jibril accompanied him

The Natural Form of Man

first from Makka to Jerusalem and then up through the Seven Heavens to the very limit of form at which Jibril himself was forced to halt although the Prophet ﷺ went on beyond into the very Presence of Allah.

The Archangel Mika'il's role in existence is all-encompassing. He is over all natural processes, the angel of creation. Everything that comes into being does so through him and the myriads of angels under him. He is, as it were, the translator of Allah's creational commands making sure that they are completely and perfectly carried out. This means, of course, that there is an angelic component, angelic participation, in everything that happens. The Prophet ﷺ made this clear in several specific statements. Every drop of rain that falls has an angel accompanying it. Every blade of grass; every budding leaf; every opening bloom; every flourishing tree. Every beast that crawls and bird that flies. Every stone and stream and valley and hill. There is nothing in existence which is not in reality imbued with angelic presence indicating and declaring its Divine provenance. It is this that has sometimes led people out of ignorance to attribute divinity to the things themselves. It is this, perceived in a heightened state, that poets and painters strive to convey through their words and on their canvasses. William Wordsworth contrives to speak for both:

> Ah! then, if mine had been the Painter's hand,
>   To express what then I saw; and add the gleam,
> The light that never was, on sea or land,
>   The consecration, and the Poet's dream.

As Mika'il is concerned with bringing things into being, Azra'il, is concerned with taking them back again. He is the Angel of Death, who takes the spirits at death and returns them to their Lord. At the appointed predetermined time he will visit every single one of us and draw our spirits out from our bodies. If we have affirmed the Divine Unity in our lives and followed Allah's guidance as brought to us by His Messengers, our spirits will slip from our bodies with no difficulty. But if we have rejected

Allah and His guidance and decided we know better, may Allah forbid, then the great reluctance of the spirit's withdrawal from the body is compared to a rusty nail being drawn with great difficulty out of a skein of tangled wool. May Allah protect us all from such an end.

Perhaps the most momentous role of all is that possessed by Israfil, the Trumpet-blower, the Angel of Annihilation. To him falls the task, when Allah's command is finally given, of causing the total annihilation of all existence, so that the Face of Allah alone remains, and then of calling it back again for the Final Account. There will be two blasts sounded by Israfil. The first will be a blast of terror announcing the arrival of the Last Day at which everything that exists will perish; and the second will call back every human being to face their reckoning. The Last Hour is always imminent. In the Qur'an Allah describes it as "*hanging heavy in the heavens and earth,*" (7:187) and the Messenger of Allah ﷺ said in reference to Israfil, "How can I give myself to enjoyment when the one with the Trumpet has raised the Trumpet to his mouth and knitted his brow and is poised to blow?" (Sa'id ibn Mansur, Ahmad, 'Abd ibn Humayd, at-Tirmidhi, Abu Ya'la, Ibn Hibban, Ibn Khuzayma, Abu ash-Shaykh, al-Hakim, al-Bayhaqi, at-Tabarani, Abu Nu'aym, al-Khatib)

Along with these four great beings there are others of similar magnitude and magnificence. There are the Throne-bearers who are mighty angels charged with the responsibility of holding up the Throne of Allah, which is the greatest of all created things. There are eight of them and they are so huge that the distance between the neck and shoulder of one of them is described as being as far as the fastest horse could travel in seven hundred years. Near these are the *Karubiyyun*, angels near to Allah whose sole function is to bask in His presence unceasingly glorifying and praising Him. There is Ridwan, chief of the beautiful angels who are the custodians of the Gardens of Paradise and his counterpart Malik, chief of the terrible angels who are the custodians of Hellfire.

The angels we have been talking about up to now have basically all been cosmic beings of universal dimensions but there are also angels of a much more intimate personal kind. Every single individual human being has attendant angels of various sorts. We each have guardian angels who are with us from birth to death, night and day, wherever we are. Their task is to protect us from harm and, whenever possible, to guide us to the good. This protection can vary from simple reminders, such as suddenly remembering we have forgotten something and many other similar things, which all of us experience on a daily basis, to more spectacular occurrences, such as when we narrowly miss being killed or escape unscathed from serious accidents, which happen to almost everyone at some time in their lives.

Angelic guidance to the human being comes in the form of inspiration to do something beneficial or prickings of conscience. The difference between it and satanic whisperings is that the latter almost invariably come with force and are concerned with self-gratification and if acted upon leave a feeling of guilt and self-disgust but if firmly denied soon go away, whereas the former, the angelic voice, is usually very soft at first and easily blocked out but if followed up becomes stronger and stronger and when acted upon leaves you with a feeling of well-being and the certain knowledge you have done the right thing. The third impulse is the voice of the human self, which can be characterised as like a tired little child endlessly whining at his mother to get his way.

Each of us also has recording angels who quite literally keep a record of every moment of our lives. This is the Book we will be presented with on the Day of Resurrection, from which nothing whatsoever will be missing and which constitutes the indisputable evidence on which our Reckoning will be based. Thus our ultimate fate in the Next World, although we only find out on the Day of Judgement what it will be, is not the result of some arbitrary decision taken then, but is rather made up of the texture of our lives in this world; we are either condemning or exonerating ourselves minute by minute and day by day and our recording angels are with us, one on each side, writing it all down.

The guardian angels exemplify one way that the angels interact with human beings, which is by means of direct inspiration when angelic influence is experienced as an inner prompting to good. However, there are other ways in which angels can and do directly impinge on human existence. One is by taking on human form.

It is impossible for angels to manifest themselves in their true form in this dimension of existence which simply would not be able to withstand the brightness of their light. Therefore when Allah wishes angels to appear in this world they appear in human form. One example of this mentioned in the Qur'an is the angels who were sent to warn Lut (Lot) of the imminent destruction of Sodom and Gomorrah. They first visited Ibrahim who realised they were angels when they did not eat the food he had prepared. Another example is the angel sent to Maryam to tell her she would give birth to 'Isa (Jesus). There were also many occasions in the Prophet's 鑾 life when Jibril appeared to him in human form.

This book is based on the famous occasion when Jibril appeared in the presence of a large gathering of the Companions. They were sitting with the Prophet 鑾 one day when a man came up and sat down right in front of him. The astonishing thing was that, although none of them knew him and therefore he could only be a newly arrived traveller, his clothes were spotlessly white and his hair shining black. He asked the Prophet 鑾 some questions and then ratified his replies which the Companions also found surprising. When he had gone the Prophet 鑾 told them he had been Jibril who had come to teach them.

There are in fact many recorded instances when people, who have found themselves in difficulties of one sort or another, have been helped by the sudden appearance of a person who has shown them a way out and subsequently disappeared without trace. There is no reason at all to doubt that in at least some

The Natural Form of Man

cases this is the result of angelic intervention in human affairs.

Another way in which angels have a direct effect on human affairs is when angelic energy makes itself felt in this world. This can take various forms. It is known from the Qur'an, for instance, that the Muslims were helped militarily by receiving angelic support in several battles during the life of the Prophet ﷺ. This appeared as lending an overwhelming violent force to the Muslims' efforts and as panic and terror in the hearts of their enemies. Examples of this particular kind of angelic reinforcement in a military context are very numerous.

One more recent occurrence happened during the fighting in Afghanistan between the Russians and the *Mujahidun*. A comparatively weakly held *Mujahidun* position (about twenty men with machine guns and a couple of mortars) was being attacked by a Russian tank platoon of greatly superior strength. Suddenly, for no apparent reason, all the tanks halted and their occupants got out and started running away as fast as they could in the opposite direction leaving the perfectly operational tanks they had been driving in *Mujahidun* hands. One of the Russians was captured and questioned about what had happened. He said that out of the blue all of them were simultaneously paralysed by a blind panic and could think of nothing but getting away as soon as possible.

There is another form of angelic energy people experience which is very different to the previous one though it too is often felt on the battlefield. That is the feeling of calm and tranquillity that sometimes comes over the heart of the believer in the middle of the most tumultuous and stressful situations. This is called in Arabic, *sakina*, stillness or tranquillity. An angelic presence can also often be clearly felt at particular holy places, like the tombs of saints and some places of worship. This can sometimes be very strong, appearing as an almost tangible densification of the atmosphere, the beating of myriad angel wings. In all of these and many other ways the angelic world intersects with ours continually.

This then has been a brief glimpse into the angelic dimensions of existence which I hope has been able to convey some sense of the reality of the angelic world and its interaction with our own. There are indeed countless more things in heaven and earth than are generally reckoned with in the narrow confines of the dominant philosophy of scientific materialism.

We cannot afford to take the false, so-called scientific, position of thinking we are impartial observers of the phenomenal world. That is the literally soul-destroying viewpoint of modern man. The truth is that the universe we inhabit is literally bursting with angels; creation is vibrant with the energy of ceaseless angelic activity. This is not in question. What is in question is us. Are we people who are able to fulfil the demands which knowledge of the angels imposes on us? It requires us to change. Having such knowledge, we can no longer afford to be passive consumers in a society which is all but explicitly dedicated to the destruction of people's spiritual well-being. We have to act on our knowledge and become true inheritors of the mantle of divine guidance which has been passed down to us, determined to see human beings restored to their rightful status as Allah's representatives on the earth with all that that entails. If we do not strive for this, we will poison and destroy our own hearts. If we do, we will truly live and die in the company of the angels, realising to the full the splendour of what it is to be a human being.

The Divine Books

The Qur'an is the last of Allah's books and within its text it refers to the phenomenon of Divine Revelation in general, and previous examples of it, on many occasions.

If they deny you, those before them also denied.
Their Messengers came to them with Clear Signs,
and written texts and the Illuminating Book. (35:25)

We have revealed to you as We revealed to Nuh
and the Prophets who came after him.
And We revealed to Ibrahim and Isma'il
and Is'haq and Ya'qub and the Tribes,
and 'Isa and Ayyub and Yunus
and Harun and Sulayman.
And We gave Dawud the Zabur.
Messengers We have already told you about
and Messengers We have not told you about.
And Allah spoke directly to Musa.
Messengers bringing good news and giving warning,
so that people will have no argument against Allah
after the coming of the Messengers.
Allah is Almighty, All-Wise. (4:162-4)

There is no doubt that one of the defining characteristics of the human being is the ability to communicate verbally. We are told in the Qur'an:

He (Allah) taught Adam the names, all of them. (2:30)

This capacity of being able to name, the gift of language, is what differentiates the human being from other creatures. A few *ayats* later we find:

Then when guidance comes to you from Me,
*   those who follow My guidance*
will feel no fear and know no sorrow. (2:37)

Because of this unique human linguistic capacity Divine guidance to the human species has taken a linguistic form. Allah says:

Then Adam received some words from His Lord
and He turned towards him. (2:36)

Throughout human history the Creator has periodically used language as the means of revealing His guidance to human communities who were in need of it. This guidance was often written down and made into Books. These Revealed Books are, therefore, a direct communication from the Creator to His human creatures in human language. For a much deeper look at the nature of this process and the way it occurs I recommend the chapter entitled the Science of Qur'an in Shaykh Abdalqadir as-Sufi's seminal text, *The Way of Muhammad.*

There have been many instances of recorded Divine Revelation since the beginning of the human story. Those mentioned in the Qur'an are a text from Ibrahim, which has been lost, the *Tawrah* of Musa, the *Zabur* of Dawud (David) and the *Injil* of 'Isa, with the Torah, Psalms and Gospels respectively containing some elements of those works although it is impossible to equate them entirely. This is clearly not an exhaustive list and there have undoubtedly been many others in different places at different times. One thing, however, which they all have in common at this point in time is that any of them which are still extant in any way exist at best in a partial and changed form and are frequently nothing more than archaeological fragments.

The only Divine Book revealed in the full light of recorded history and known to be unaltered in any way is the Qur'an, the final Divine Revelation revealed to the last of the Messengers, Muhammad ﷺ and dictated by him to his Companions who memorised it and wrote it down and preserved it for all posterity. So it is worth a more detailed look at the Qur'an itself to gain a greater understanding of what Divine communication to human beings entails. We find in it:

> [Say:] This Qur'an has been revealed to me
> so that I may warn you by it,
>   and anyone else it reaches. (6:19)

> This Qur'an guides to the most upright Way
> and gives good news to the believers. (17:9)

> We tell you the best of stories in revealing this Qur'an to you,
>   even though you were unaware of it before it came. (12:2-3)

> We send down in the Qur'an that which is a healing
> and a mercy to the believers. (17:82)

All Muslims are aware of the supreme importance of the Qur'an and consider it the greatest miracle of the Messenger of Allah ﷺ. It contains the Guidance from Allah which he was sent to transmit to the human race and which he implemented and demonstrated throughout the course of his life as a Prophet ﷺ among his Companions in Makka and Madina.

The indispensable key to understanding the Qur'an is to grasp that in it you are addressed directly by the Lord of the Universe, and that Muhammad ﷺ was sent in order that this address should reach you. This is the outstanding nature of the Qur'anic miracle.

First, putting aside the exquisite beauty of its language and the supreme eloquence of its means of expression, if we wish to gain greater insight into the nature of Divine Revelation it is necessary for us to be aware of the meaning of what it contains, and what is considered necessary for human beings to know. The scholars of Islam have traditionally divided the contents of the Qur'an into three parts. These are not hard and fast divisions but indicate the three main topics with which it deals. They have defined these as *tawhid, qasas* and *ahkam*: in other words the Divine Unity, stories of the Prophets and legal judgements. Each of these divisions covers a wide area and none of them is mutually exclusive. And we must always bear in mind that the Revelation in the end defies any attempt at precise analysis or exact definition of any sort.

TAWHID – DIVINE UNITY

The part dealing with the Divine Unity first and foremost tells us what we can know about Allah Himself and includes the passages in *Surat al-Ikhlas, Ayat al-Kursi,* the beginning of *Surat al-Hadid,* which we already looked at in the chapter on *iman,* and the end of *Surat al-Hashr* which follows:

> *He is Allah – there is no god but Him.*
> *He is the Knower of the Unseen and the Visible.*
> *He is the All-Merciful, the Most Merciful.*
> *He is Allah – there is no god but Him.*
> *He is the King, the Most Pure, the Perfect Peace,*
> *the Trustworthy, the Safeguarder, the Almighty,*
> *the Compeller, the Supremely Great.*
> *Glory be to Allah above all they associate with Him.*
> *He is Allah – the Creator, the Maker, the Giver of Form.*
> *To Him belong the Most Beautiful Names.*
> *Everything in the heavens and earth glorifies Him.*
> *He is the Almighty, the All-Wise.* (59:22-24)

There are, of course, many other *ayats* which deal directly with the nature of the Divine Reality. They tell us everything we need to know about our Lord and Creator. Alongside these are the arguments for the Divine Existence. *Surat al-An'am* is full of these including the famous passage about the Prophet Ibrahim ﷺ:

Remember when Ibrahim said to his father, Azar,
    'Do you take idols as gods?
  I see that you and your people are clearly misguided.'
Because of that We showed Ibrahim
    the dominions of the heavens and the earth
      so that he might be one of the people of certainty.
When night covered him he saw a star and said,
    'This is my Lord!'
  Then when it set he said,
    'I do not love what sets.'
Then when he saw the moon come up he said,
    'This is my Lord!'
  Then when it set he said,
    'If my Lord does not guide me,
      I will be one of the misguided people.'
Then when he saw the sun come up he said,
    'This is my Lord! This is greater!'
  Then when it set he said,
    'My people, I am free of what
      you associate with Allah!
    I have turned my face to Him
  who brought the heavens and earth into being,
    a pure natural believer.
  I am not one of the mushrikun.'
His people argued with him.
  He said, 'Are you arguing with me about Allah
    when He has guided me?
  I have no fear of any partner you ascribe to Him
    unless my Lord should will such a thing to happen.
  My Lord encompasses all things in His knowledge
    so will you not pay heed?
  Why should I fear what you have associated with Him
    when you yourselves apparently have no fear
      of associating with Allah partners
      for which He has sent down no authority to you?

Which of the two parties is more entitled to feel safe,
  if you have any knowledge?'

This is the argument We gave to Ibrahim
  against his people.
We raise in rank anyone We will.
  Your Lord is All-Wise, All-Knowing. (6:75-84)

Such arguments occur in many other places as well. However, this aspect of the Qur'an extends far beyond this and tells us about the nature of existence as a whole and of the universe we inhabit. We are told all about the unseen realms of angelic power. We are told in many ways about the Last Day and the accounting process that takes place on it and are given detailed and graphic descriptions of the Garden and the Fire. One comprehensive passage on this theme is to be found in *Surat al-Haqqa*:

So when the Trumpet is blown
  with a single blast,
and the earth and the mountains
  are lifted and crushed
    with a single blow,
On that Day, the Occurrence will occur
  and Heaven will be split apart,
    for that Day it will be very frail.
The angels will be gathered round its edge.
  On that Day, eight will bear the Throne of their Lord
    above their heads.
On that Day you will be exposed –
  no concealed act you did
    will stay concealed.
As for him who is given his Book in his right hand,
  he will say, 'Here, come and read my Book!
    I counted on meeting my Reckoning.'
He will have a very pleasant life
  in an elevated Garden,
    its ripe fruit hanging close to hand.

'Eat and drink with relish
  for what you did before in days gone by!'
But as for him who is given his Book in his left hand,
  he will say, 'If only I had not been given my Book
    and had not known about my Reckoning!
If only death had really been the end!
  My wealth has been of no use to me.
    My power has vanished.'
'Seize him and truss him up.
  Then roast him in the Blazing Fire.
  Then bind him in a chain
    which is seventy cubits long.
He used not to believe in Allah the Most Great,
  nor did he urge the feeding of the poor.
Therefore here today he has no friend
  nor any food except exuding pus
    which no one will eat except those
      who were in error.' (69:12-36)

Among the physical sciences alluded to by the Book are
physics, biology, astronomy, geology and meteorology. Both the
plant world and the animal world are mentioned in some detail.

It is He Who sends down water from the sky
  from which We bring forth growth of every kind,
and from that We bring forth the green shoots
  and from them We bring forth close-packed seeds,
and from the spathes of the date palm
  date clusters hanging down,
and gardens of grapes and olives and pomegranates,
  both similar and dissimilar.
Look at their fruits as they bear fruit and ripen.
  There are Signs in that for people who believe. (6:100)

And He created livestock.
  There is warmth for you in them,
    and various uses

and some you eat.
And there is beauty in them for you
in the evening
when you bring them home
and in the morning
when you drive them out to graze.
They carry your loads to lands
you would never reach
except with great difficulty.
Your Lord is All-Gentle, Most Merciful.
And horses, mules and donkeys
both to ride and for adornment.
And He creates other things you do not know. (16:5-8)

In the Qur'an Allah also refers in some detail to the growth process, the weather cycle and many other matters we know about the world we live in, drawing lessons from them:

Mankind, if you are in any doubt about the Rising,
know that We created you from dust
then from a drop of sperm
then from a clot of blood
then from a lump of flesh,
formed yet unformed,
so We may make things clear to you.
We make whatever We want stay in the womb
until a specified time
and then We bring you out as children
so that you can reach your full maturity.
Some of you die
and some of you revert to the lowest form of life
so that, after having knowledge,
they then know nothing at all.
And you see the earth dead and barren;
then when We send down water onto it
it quivers and swells

and sprouts with luxuriant plants of every kind. (22:5)

Do you not see that Allah propels the clouds
  then makes them coalesce
    then heaps them up,
  and then you see the rain come pouring
    out of the middle of them?
And He sends down mountains from the sky
  with hail inside them,
  striking with it anyone He wills
    and averting it from anyone He wills.
The brightness of His lightning almost blinds the sight.
  Allah revolves night and day.
There is surely a lesson in that
  for people with inner sight. (24:42)

Allah informs us about how all these things relate to their Creator and most importantly that in reality everything which happens is the act of Allah alone and this is the essence of a true understanding of the Divine Unity.

QASAS –STORIES

The part dealing with *qasas* or stories is limited in many people's minds to the stories of ancient peoples, such as 'Ad and Thamud, and their Prophets, mentioned particularly in *Surat al-A'raf* and *Sura Hud* but also found right through the whole Qur'an from beginning to end. It does, of course, include these and from them we gain much knowledge particularly of the besetting vices which corrupt human societies and eventually bring about their destruction. It is significant that all of them seem to be prevalent in the world today. The following refers in general to all such peoples:

These cities – We have given you news of them.
  Their Messengers came to them with Clear Signs,
    but they were never going to believe
      in what they had previously rejected.

That is how Allah seals up the hearts of the unbelievers.
We did not find many of them worthy of their contract.
We found most of them to be deviators. (7:100-1)

But in fact the *qasas* – stories – cover far more than just that. First of all they give us a complete understanding of human history, which turns upside down the Darwinian historical perspective with which all of us have been have been thoroughly indoctrinated. This alone is a huge lesson to grasp.

The various recountings of the story of Musa and Pharaoh give us, along with much other knowledge, a comprehensive picture of human political possibilities. Musa's dealings with the tribe of Israel and what we learn about them give us a great insight into the geopolitical situation of the world today, if we study them carefully. Then we have the accounts relating to Adam, Ibrahim, Yusuf (Joseph), Dawud, Sulayman (Solomon) and 'Isa and other Prophets and people of the past all of which contain untold instruction for us.

Very importantly, also under this heading come the many passages dealing with what happened during the life of the Prophet ﷺ and his Companions, the archetypical nature of which is made clear to us. Allah draws out every drop of wisdom for us from the very texture of the events themselves so that the lessons they teach are equally as applicable and useful for our own lives today as they were then, to the extent that there is scarcely any state or predicament a human being can get into which is not prefigured and resolved in the text of the Qur'an. One among many such passages is this one in *Sura Ali 'Imran* referring to an incident in the Battle of Uhud:

Remember when you were scrambling up the slope,
  refusing to turn back for anyone,
and the Messenger was calling to you from the rear.
  Allah rewarded you with one distress
    in return for another
  so you would not feel grief for what escaped you

or what assailed you.
Allah is aware of what you do.
Then He sent down to you, after the distress, security,
    restful sleep overtaking a group of you,
   whereas another group became prey to anxious thoughts,
    thinking other than the truth about Allah –
       thoughts belonging to the Time of Ignorance –
    saying, 'Do we have any say in the affair at all?'
    Say, 'The affair belongs entirely to Allah.'
They are concealing things inside themselves
    which they do not disclose to you,
    saying, 'If we had only had a say in the affair,
    none of us would have been killed here in this place.'
Say, 'Even if you had been inside your homes,
    those people for whom killing was decreed
    would have gone out to their place of death.'
So that Allah might test what is in your breasts
    and purge what is in your hearts.
Allah knows the contents of your hearts. (3:153-4)

Finally and vitally it is in this part that Allah instructs us in those qualities of character which mark out the believers and are indispensable for gaining His pleasure and tells us of those which characterise the unbelievers and hypocrites and which we must strive to get rid of. An example of such a passage is:

It is the believers who are successful:
    those who are humble in their prayer;
    those who turn away from worthless talk;
    those who actively pay zakat;
    those who guard their private parts –
       except from their wives or those they own as slaves,
       in which case they are not blameworthy;
       but those who desire anything more than that
       are people who have gone beyond the limits –
    those who honour their trusts and their contracts;

those who safeguard their prayers:
such people are the inheritors
who inherit Paradise,
remaining in it timelessly, forever. (23:1-11)

AHKAM – LEGAL JUDGEMENTS

The third division, comprising *ahkam* or legal judgements, is also much more extensive than it is often reckoned to be. It is by no means restricted to those *ayats* which lay down the specifics of Islamic law governing the pillars of Islam, the permitted and forbidden, marriage and divorce, inheritance, property law, commercial transactions, warfare and criminal offices, although they, of course, form its core and contain everything we need to govern every aspect of our lives:

And We have sent down the Book to you with truth,
confirming and conserving the previous Books.
So judge between them by what Allah has sent down
and do not follow their whims and desires
deviating from the Truth that has come to you.
We have appointed a law and a practice
for every one of you.
Had Allah willed,
He would have made you a single community,
but He wanted to test you regarding what has come to you.
So compete with each other in doing good.
Every one of you will return to Allah
and He will inform you regarding the things
about which you differed.
Judge between them by what Allah has sent down
and do not follow their whims and desires.
And beware of them lest they lure you away
from some of what Allah has sent down to you.
If they turn their backs, then know that Allah
wants to afflict them with some of their wrong actions.
Many of mankind are deviators.

Do they then seek the judgement of the Time of Ignorance?
Who could be better at giving judgement than Allah
for people with certainty? (5:48-50)

Ahkam also includes such passages as those in *Suras al-An'am* and *Isra* and the beginning of *Surat al-Muminun* and the end of *Surat al-Furqan* which give the outline of the ancient *deen* which underlies the specifics of its final form in the Islamic *shari'a*.

The slaves of the All-Merciful are those
who walk lightly on the earth
and, who, when the ignorant speak to them,
say, 'Peace';
those who pass the night
prostrating and standing before their Lord;
those who say, 'Our Lord,
avert from us the punishment of Hell,
its punishment is inescapable pain.
It is indeed an evil lodging and abode';
those who, when they spend,
are neither extravagant nor mean,
but take a stance mid way between the two;
those who do not call on
any other god together with Allah
and do not kill anyone Allah has forbidden,
except with the right to do so,
and do not fornicate;
anyone who does that will receive an evil punishment
and on the Day of Rising
his punishment will be doubled
and he will be humiliated in it timelessly, for ever,
except for those who make tawba
and believe and act rightly:
Allah will transform the wrong actions
of such people into good
– Allah is Ever-Forgiving, Most Merciful –

for certainly all who make tawba and act rightly
have turned sincerely towards Allah;
those who do not bear false witness
and who, when they pass by worthless talk,
pass by with dignity;
those who, when they are reminded
of the Signs of their Lord,
do not turn their backs, deaf and blind to them;
those who say, 'Our Lord,
give us joy in our wives and children
and make us a good example
for those who have taqwa;'
such people will be repaid for their steadfastness
with the Highest Paradise,
where they will meet with welcome and with 'Peace'.
They will remain in it timelessly, for ever.
What an excellent lodging and abode! (25:63-76)

Also within its compass are the many *ayats* addressed directly to the believers containing all sorts of instructions and prohibitions which may not necessarily be legal injunctions but which nonetheless govern our behaviour to a considerable extent.

This then has been a general rundown of the classical formulation of the contents of Allah's Book but it would be absurd to assert that it covers them completely. There is much, much more. Its contents are inexhaustible. It contains everything people need for their lives in this world and the Next. Allah says in it:

We have not omitted anything from the Book. (6:38)

So far the discussion has been confined to the contents of the Qur'an but now we turn to what the Qur'an actually is. We find in it the *ayat*:

If We Had sent down this Qur'an onto a mountain,
you would have seen it humbled,

crushed to pieces out of fear of Allah.
We make such examples for people
so that hopefully they will reflect. (59:21)

What then is this Book whose descent is so powerful that it would smash a mountain to bits? This is a question which very few Muslims seem to ask any more but it is something which the early Muslims cared passionately about. What happened that night in the cave of Hira when Allah's Messenger ﷺ received the first revelation? Words were brought to the Prophet ﷺ by the Angel Jibril, peace be upon him, directly from Allah, glory be to Him, which took the form of Arabic letters and words and emerged as the sentence:

Recite: In the Name of your Lord Who created,
created man from clots of blood. (96:1-2)

What we have to realise is that this cataclysmic event is from any rational standpoint completely impossible. Something directly from the Creator of the Universe Who is beyond form, and cannot be contained by any form, somehow entered into the form of letters and words which were etched upon the heart of the Prophet Muhammad ﷺ and then emerged on his tongue out into this world. In some way, which is beyond our capacity to comprehend, something directly from Allah Himself descended into this world; the timeless came into time; the infinite somehow became finite in the words of the Qur'an. A famous classical definition expresses it thus: the Qur'an is the real word of Allah and is neither created nor originated in time; it is recited by our tongues, written in books and preserved in our breasts but does not dwell in them.

This subject was a matter of passionate debate for many years in the early centuries of Islam. Imam Ahmad ibn Hanbal, was beaten daily for months and months for following the path of the noble *salaf* – the right-acting first generations – and refusing to bow to the dictates of the rationalists and assert that the Qur'an was created. There can be no answer to the question "how?" about the exact nature of the Qur'an just as there can be no "how?" about the nature of the Divine Essence. The point is that it happened.

Something of the momentous nature of the event can be gleaned from what happened to the Prophet ﷺ when the Revelation came to him, and remember that he was created for it and prepared by Allah to receive it. We know that the first time it came he was twice crushed to the point of death. On other occasions it is reported that his weight increased dramatically at the time when *ayats* were being revealed and that he sweated profusely even on cold days. Abu Bakr as-Siddiq ﷺ showed that he understood what was happening when he said when questioned about the Prophet's ﷺ Night Journey to Jerusalem: "If he says it happened it is true. He tells me that Revelation comes down to him in no time at all right from Heaven to Earth during both day and night and that is a far greater matter than that which you are carping at." (Al-Mustadrak of al-Hakim)

The Qur'an is something tremendous beyond anything we can possibly know. Every letter, every syllable, in it has come directly from the presence of Allah, the unknowable who is All-knowing, the formless who is All-Encompassing, the Creator of the universe and of each one of us and all our actions.

A taste of the awesome reality of Allah's words in His Book was once brought home to me by a man of great knowledge in Morocco when I was living there shortly after I became Muslim. He asked me if I had read and understood the Qur'an. I said that I had an English translation and had done my best to match it up with the Arabic. He said to me, "No, I don't mean that. Have you really understood the Qur'an." "What do mean then by understand?" I asked. "If you were truly to understand even a single letter of the Qur'an," he replied, "you would scarcely eat or sleep for forty days because of the light that is in it. I know this," he continued, "because it happened to me." This is the truth about the Qur'an; every *ayat* is potentially more powerful than any weapon; every letter a possible window onto the very Face of Allah.

Divine Messengers

to believe in the Divine Messengers...

We sent a Messenger among every people saying:
"Worship Allah and keep clear of false gods."
Among them were some whom Allah guided
but others got the misguidance they deserved.
So travel in the land
and see the end result of the deniers. (16:36)

We have revealed to you as We revealed to Nuh
and the Prophets who came after him.
And We revealed to Ibrahim and Isma'il
and Is'haq and Ya'qub and the Tribes,
and 'Isa and Ayyub and Yunus
and Harun and Sulayman.
And We gave Dawud the Zabur.
Messengers We have already told you about
and Messengers We have not told you about.
And Allah spoke directly to Musa.
Messengers bringing good news and giving warning,
so that people will have no argument against Allah
after the coming of the Messengers.
Allah is Almighty, All-Wise. (6:162-4)

HISTORICAL PERSPECTIVE

To understand the full implications that belief in the Prophets
and Messengers entails, it is basically necessary to turn on its head

the historical perspective which all of us have had drummed into us from our earliest years. We have to jettison the almost universally held modern hypothesis that we have now reached the summit of a slow and laborious process of evolution during the course of which the human creature somehow emerged out of a remote bestial past into a savage prehuman and then into the supposedly "advanced", "civilised" creature of this time. As with many myths of this kind, quite the reverse is true.

It is true that the surface of the earth was made ready to receive the human being and that this happened in several quite clearly defined stages. What is not true is that human beings evolved out of other animal forms. The early accounts are true, the later ones fabricated. The human creature was created complete and perfect and with a totally different function to anything else in existence.

Everything else was created to fulfil a limited defined role in creation in unconscious submission to the complex network of laws that governed its existence. The human being on the other hand, by virtue of faculties not present in any other creature, has the capacity to comprehend existence and therefore by extension worship the Creator of the universe. Human beings were created to recognise and worship their Creator and Lord. That is why we are here. Everything else was created to make this possible.

However it is in the nature of things that human beings are prone to lose sight of their true nature and fall prey to a short-sighted absorption in the world that surrounds them, becoming in the process virtually indistinguishable from animals, and on occasions considerably worse. But because our Creator is inexhaustibly merciful and desires the best for His creatures, human history was punctuated by the expression of that mercy in the form of Messengers and Prophets from Allah to His human creatures. These were men inspired directly by Allah Himself to recall their fellow men to the Truth, reminding them that worship of Allah is the cornerstone of their existence, and restoring the harmonious and just social situation which is the inevitable outcome when human beings live in tune with their real nature.

Not one human community was left without guidance and the stories of those who brought and rebrought this guidance from their Lord – a guidance which was in each case essentially the same but which varied in certain respects according to the particular time and place – follow a largely recognisable pattern. They appeared in communities which had either not previously received revealed guidance or who had received it in the past and then neglected it and fallen into decadence.

Their call to their fellows was largely ignored and frequently ridiculed since they affirmed the power of Allah, which is invisible, against the power structure of their society, which was all that was manifest to their people. In the face of continual opposition, frequently accompanied by physical persecution, they persevered in their task of delivering Allah's message that there is no god except Him and that justice and harmony in human society are only possible when this is recognised and put into practice, following the example of the Messenger ﷺ and those who were sent before him.

After a time they usually succeeded in gathering around them a larger or smaller group of followers, often from among the poor and oppressed in their society. Finally, in the face of the continuing obduracy of those who opposed them, they were inspired to deliver warnings of the inevitable destruction of those who stand against the power of Allah. This was generally to little avail with the result that that society was wiped out with the exception of the Messenger and his band of followers who survived to form the basis of a new community. In its turn, this new community expanded and flourished under the guidance of the Messenger and his immediate successors until it in its turn went the way of the previous communities into decline and decadence. Then once more another Prophet would be sent and the story repeat itself again.

This cycle of renewal, growth and decay occurring in conjunction with the appearance of envoys from Allah, mirroring as it does all natural processes, is the true picture of human history. There is no steady unbroken line of "evolution", "progress" or "advancement" as the modem myth-makers would have us believe. Rather there have been a great number of these human cycles, some simple and unpretentious, others of unbelievable complexity and sophistication, stretching right back to the very beginning of the human story.

The number of those sent by Allah in the course of the span of human history to bring His guidance and re-imbue human communities with justice and moral parameters is certainly very great and reckoned by some traditional authorities to be one hundred and twenty-four thousand. It is obviously beyond our scope here to enumerate all of them, but it would be useful to look briefly at those who form, as it were, the landmarks of human history as we know it. These pivotal human beings, around whom the whole human story revolves, are Adam, Nuh (Noah), Ibrahim, Musa, 'Isa and Muhammad ﷺ.

Adam was at once the first prophet and the first man and progenitor of the human race. His story contains and prefigures the story of his descendants. Unfortunately the Christian view of what happened completely misses the point and contains elements that were to work great mischief. There was no original sin, nor did woman cause the fall of man. The story of Adam is the story of the unfolding of the human creature. The important part of the story is not the fall of Adam and Hawwa (Eve) from the Garden. The important part of this story is their regaining the Mercy of Allah by means of the faculty of language and knowledge of the "Names" with which his Lord had endowed him. The fall was the necessary manifestation of the frailty of human nature, the process of veiling which must necessarily take place if guidance is to be gained. In this lies the whole secret and indeed the whole point of human existence.

Nuh marks the end of the first people, the ancients, and at

the same time his story demonstrates in an archetypal way the prophetic pattern referred to above. He called his people to the truth for nine and a half centuries and was ignored and mocked by them. In the end his guidance took the physical form of the ark and he was literally entrusted with the reintroduction of human life, and animal life for that matter, to the surface of the earth. The people of his time were totally destroyed by the Flood, while he and his family and those who followed him by virtue of the guidance he received from his Lord floated free and began literally all over again.

Ibrahim also plays a vital part in the human story. The people of his time had once more become completely engrossed in, and blinded by, material existence until there was no one left practising pure worship of Allah. He was chosen by Allah and inspired directly by Him with a true understanding of the nature of the universe until he gained certain knowledge of the One God Who is the Creator and Sustainer of everything in existence. He was the one chosen by Allah to bring back to mankind the knowledge of the Unity of Allah and he is the father both literally and metaphorically of all surviving true religious traditions. Literally because many of those who upheld and defended this unitarian belief, including both 'Isa and Muhammad, were his direct descendants, and metaphorically because all teachings containing the unitarian doctrine stem from his reaffirmation of Allah's unity.

The story of Musa is again of immense significance for us as people of this time. In his confrontation with the monolithic power structure of Pharaonic Egypt there are many vital lessons for us, since the system which confronts us today is based on exactly the same principles. Much insight into our own situation can be gained from examining the details of the encounter between Musa and Pharaoh. The second half of Musa's story deals with his relationship with his people, the Banu Isra'il (The Children or Tribe of Israel). In the picture of these people which emerges from this story lies a key to the situation existing in the world today. Their excessive love of this world, epitomised by their making the Golden Calf and their desire for what they had left behind in Egypt, is the hallmark of all those who have pursued power in the world ever since and has played a large part in the political and economic landscape of our time. It could be said that Musa marks the beginning of the modem and final age.

'Isa was the last of the Prophets sent to the Banu Isra'il. He sealed the prophetic descent from Ibrahim in that line, although by the fact of his having no father from the Tribe of Isra'il, in a manner he stood outside of them, always speaking to them as "O Tribe of Isra'il" rather than employing the form of address of the other Prophets "O my people". His having no father and no descendants indicated his finality as a Messenger among them, something that was unthinkable to the Children of Isra'il, who had always had Prophets who were the descendants of previous Prophets among them.

His real function was to revive and purify the teaching of Musa among the Banu Isra'il but, as we know, Paul, who never met 'Isa, invented the religion of Christianity based on certain personal visionary experiences. After this already altered version of the prophethood of 'Isa had been subjected to Greek philosophical principles and Roman pragmatism, both heavily tinged with outright paganism, and had then been further compromised by unscrupulous powerbrokers, it was far removed from its original purity. It was nevertheless, despite the perversion and many changes, based on the prophetic model and because of this tenuous relationship was able to support the civilisation which grew up under the name of Christendom.

At the same time because of the fundamental changes that were made to the original teaching, such as the attribution of divinity to 'Isa and the absorption of the trinitarian thesis from Greek philosophy, Christendom proved powerless in the face of the onslaught of scientific materialism in the guise of humanism. Its collapse has led to the moral and social disintegration we find ourselves in today. From the story of the Prophet 'Isa we can clearly see how prophetic inspiration forms the basis of social renewal and how at the same time it becomes corrupted and in need of rejuvenation.

The final renewal of the prophetic tradition was the function of the last Prophet and Messenger Muhammad ﷺ, and it is in this perspective of constantly renewed Divine guidance that we must view the story of Muhammad's ﷺ life. It was not an isolated event but rather the culmination of a lengthy series of repeatedly renewed Divine Revelations. The finality of the prophethood of Muhammad ﷺ makes it, of course, relevant to us in a way that is not the case in any of the previous revelations, since by virtue of its lastness it contains the final instructions from the Creator to His creatures. Because of this, Allah has ensured that it has remained accessible to us in every detail both as regards the actual revealed Book, the Noble Qur'an, and as regards the implementation of the revelation in the life of Muhammad and his Companions.

THE NATURE OF PROPHETHOOD

It is only through the reality of prophethood that we have access to knowledge of Allah's unity and, since the whole purpose of all human existence is to know and worship Allah, the sole means we now have of accomplishing this is, therefore, by believing in the Messengership of Muhammad ﷺ and following the Message he brought. Were it not for the fact that he brought us the Message and showed us how to apply it to our lives the human race would be living in darkness, in a mire of misguidance and confusion. As Shaykh Ibn Mashish so eloquently put it: 'If it was not for the means, the end, as they say, would have escaped us.' (as-Salat al-Mashishiyyah) This means that belief in the Prophet ﷺ has the same importance as belief in Allah Himself.

But what exactly constitutes belief in the Messengers of Allah? We know that in His limitless knowledge Allah predetermined that a few among all the countless human beings He would create would have the glorious but burdensome destiny of being

Prophets and Messengers of Allah. They would be responsible for delivering His Messages to mankind and guiding them to the Straight Path which leads to human fulfilment and success in both this world and the Next.

In an *ayat* of Qur'an, Allah, exalted is He, says, "*I only created jinn and man to worship Me.*" (51:52) Worship in this *ayat* was interpreted by the Companion Ibn 'Abbas 🙵 to mean "to have knowledge (*ma'rifa*) of" in the sense of the gnostic recognition of Allah. This was the reason for the creation of the world. In other words it was the desire to be known expressed in the depths of the Essence of the Divine Unity that brought about the beginning of the process of creation and led to the unfolding of the many layers of existence and all the forms contained in them including the earth with all its mineral, plant, and animal life.

At a certain point, when the environment was completely prepared for it, a new creature was brought into existence – man. Until this event, all the different forms of existence had varying degrees of awareness, but man was given, by his Creator and Lord, the ability to recognise, not only his physical environment, but also that he was an inseparable part of One Reality which he perceived in himself and in everything around him. He was the summit and perfection of the whole creation and the means by which the Lord of creation would achieve His desire to be known.

Deep in the being of man is a secret breathed into him by his Lord which opens out onto the Majesty and Beauty of the Divine Unity. That secret is contained in the human heart which is the instrument of knowledge in general and of this gnostic knowledge in particular, and upon whose health depends the entire well-being of the human being. Muhammad 🙵 said, "Certainly in the body there is a morsel of flesh, which when it is well the entire body is well, and when it is corrupt the entire body is corrupt: it is the heart." (Al-Bukhari, Muslim)

We find in the Qur'an: "*We offered the trust to the heavens and the earth and the mountains, but they refused to carry it and were afraid of it and man carried it. Surely he is wrong-acting, very foolish."* (33:72) This wrong action and foolishness on the part of man led him to forget his true nature and to lose his awareness of the Divine Unity. He became more and more involved with the perception of his senses and, gradually, gave intrinsic reality to created forms. However, because of the Mercy inherent in the Divine Reality, men appeared among the different human communities to show them what had been lost and restore man to his true nature.

It is these men who were the Prophets and Messengers of Allah and they were created for this purpose alone. Although they were men among men, they were from their birth endowed with unobscured perception of the Divine Reality and knowledge of how to live in harmony with the Lord of the Universe. They were charged with passing on that knowledge to those around them who floundered in the darkness of forgetfulness and increasing ignorance. These Prophets and Messengers brought for their communities the guidance and direction they needed and served as examples for them, bringing them back to the worship and recognition of their Lord, the One Reality. They represent the perfection of the human creature, unspoiled by their contact with this existence, constantly aware of the Presence of their Lord. The first of them was the first man, Adam, and they continued to appear throughout the history of man on earth until the chain was completed with the coming of the Seal of the Prophets, Muhammad ﷺ. The Qur'an says: *"Muhammad is not the father of anyone of your men, but he is the Messenger of Allah and the Seal of the Prophets."* (33:40)

We have seen that the summit and fulfilment of the process of creation is in man. Although he was the last to appear, everything that preceded him was in preparation for him – the means by which the Lord of the Universe would come to know Himself. As we noted earlier it was the desire for this self-knowledge which brought about the whole unfolding of creation, and so the first impulse became a reality in the final form. In man firstness and lastness are joined together. If you desire a fruit, you must first plant a tree and then wait for it to grow, blossom, and finally, to bear fruit. However, the idea of plucking the fruit preceded the planting of the tree.

The perfection of man was embodied in the Prophets and Messengers who were the models and examples for the rest of mankind and were those in whom the Divine Unity was most perfectly reflected. They correspond most closely to the original desire in the Divine Essence for self-revelation and are, therefore, the first beings in the unfolding of the creation. As lastness and firstness are combined in man, the last of creatures, so they are combined in Muhammad ﷺ, the last of the Messengers.

BELIEF IN THE MESSENGERS

Following on from this, the scholars of Islam have carefully defined what belief in the Prophets and Messengers involves. Namely that all the Prophets from Adam to Muhammad, may Allah bless all of them and grant them peace, were utterly truthful and trustworthy and they conveyed everything they were commanded to convey to creation. All human perfection was theirs by necessity and all human imperfections were impossible for them. Permitted for them were eating, drinking, marriage, trading, and any illness which does not lead to any imperfection.

If we reflect on these words and on the statements Allah makes about His Messengers in the Qur'an, we come to understand that, while the Prophets clearly are human beings – and indeed it would not make any sense, or indeed be possible, for human guidance to come via any other means – they are, nevertheless, quite different from the ordinary run of humanity. They are very definitely special beings, set apart from the rest of mankind, protected from the faults to which all the rest of us are prone. As the last of them, as the 'Seal of the Prophets', as their apogee and their culmination, Muhammad ﷺ has an extra special place as "the best of all creation". The great poet of the Companions, Hassan ibn Thabit, put the whole matter most beautifully and succinctly in verses of a poem he wrote in praise of the Prophet ﷺ:

> Muhammad is a human being
>> but not like other human beings.
> Rather he is a flawless diamond
>> and everyone else simply stones.

It is vital to realise exactly what this implies in order that our belief in the Messengers should not be defective and consequently the whole *deen* threatened by misunderstanding the true nature of the prophetic phenomenon. Certainly it is quite clear that the reason that the adherents of the two previous Divine dispensations, the Jews and the Christians, have gone wrong was precisely their failure to grasp the true nature of prophethood.

The Jews belittled and undervalued their Prophets and Messengers. They made the mistake of diminishing their status and of considering them the same as themselves, saying, "They are human beings, just the same as we are." They did it with their own Prophets, with 'Isa and again with the last Messenger ﷺ in Madina. This led them to the worst possible human destiny, that of rejecting and, on occasion even murdering, those sent by Allah to guide them. We find in the Qur'an:

> *We will write down what they said*
>> *and their killing of the Prophets*
>>> *without any right to do so*
> *and We will say,*
>> *'Taste the punishment of the Burning.'* (3:181)

The Christians, on the other hand, made exactly the opposite mistake. They elevated their Messenger beyond the realms of human existence and by doing that made it impossible to follow him. They put between themselves and the man who had been sent to guide them a gulf which it was humanly impossible to cross. By overvaluing their Messenger, the Christians, in fact, negated the very thing he had, in reality, been sent to do. Allah says about them in the Qur'an:

> *Those who say that the Messiah,*
> *son of Maryam, is Allah*
> *are disbelievers.*
> *The Messiah said, 'Tribe of Israel! worship Allah,*
> *my Lord and your Lord.*
> *If anyone associates anything with Allah,*
> *Allah has forbidden him the Garden*
> *and his refuge will be the Fire.'*
> *The wrongdoers will have no helpers.* (5:72)

It is clear from these *ayats* that to misevaluate the nature of prophethood in these ways will have terrible consequences in the Next World but its results also inevitably manifest themselves in this world.

Misunderstanding the nature of the Messenger makes it impossible to implement the Message he brought. So the Jews turned their religion into a rigid compilation of rules and regulations in which compassion has little place. They created a nihilistic structure devoid of true spirituality which leads inevitably to injustice and self-destruction. Christianity, on the other hand, became a kind of fuzzy, personal mysticism detached from day-to-day life leading step by step to moral chaos, economic injustice, social deprivation and secular rule.

Now, it is clear that, although this misunderstanding of the nature of prophethood finds its most explicit expression among the Jews and Christians, there are also many Muslims who veer towards one or other of these two deviant positions. It is for this reason that Allah revealed the *Fatiha* for daily recitation in the prayer, containing as it does the supplication that we not deviate in the same way as did these two communities: "...*not of those with anger on them, nor of the misguided.*" (1:7)

These two tendencies, that of either underrating or overrating the stature of the Messenger of Allah ﷺ, are all too apparent among the Muslims in the world today and not only do such people espouse these erroneous positions but also, unfortunately, at the same time vehemently claim that they alone have a correct understanding of the nature of prophethood.

It is small wonder that with such people holding sway the Muslims are as far away as ever from seeing the *deen* of the Prophet ﷺ and his Companions, may Allah be pleased with all of them, implemented once more in the world. The great Muslim scholar and judge, Qadi 'Iyad al-Yahsubi (1083-1149 CE), who was acutely aware of how previous *deens* had been corrupted and could see how the same was happening to the Muslims, wrote his book, *ash-Shifa*, (published in English under the title, *Muhammad, Messenger of Allah*) precisely to give people a correct, traditional and balanced view of the nature of their Messenger ﷺ and it is essential reading for those who wish to deepen their understanding of what it means to believe in the Prophets and Messengers of Allah.

THE LAST DAY

*O*n the Day the Hour arrives,
    that day they will be split up.
    As for those who believed and did right actions,
they will be made joyful in a verdant meadow.
But as for those who disbelieved and denied Our Signs
    and the meeting of the Next World,
they will be summoned to the punishment. (30:13-15)

From one point of view belief in the Last Day is the absolute
crux of the matter; it is what human life is all about; it is the
whole point of our existence. If we have belief in it we have got
the point and if we fail to have belief in it we have missed the
point completely. Allah says in the Qur'an that the people of
true intelligence, of deep insight, say to Allah:

'Our Lord, You have not created this for nothing.
    Glory be to You!
So safeguard us from the punishment of the Fire.' (3:191)

By saying this they are clearly indicating that the purpose of
Allah's creation is in order that human beings may be judged for
their actions in this world, which will result for them in either
the reward of the Garden or the punishment of the Fire. There
is no page of the Qur'an in which people are not reminded
either implicitly or explicitly of the Day when we will be called
to account for our actions during our lives in this world. Indeed,

it is only the fact of accountability which gives meaning to the words "right" and "wrong". "Right" is what is pleasing to Allah and leads to the Garden and "wrong" is what is displeasing to Allah and leads to the Fire.

Without this accountability there is no basis for moral values. This is why the world we live in is in such moral turmoil and why the back-to-basics campaign and similar initiatives attempting to bring moral standards back to today's society are inevitably doomed to failure. It is impossible for them to be anything but empty rhetoric because it is only in the context of belief in the Divine Reality and the Last Day that the language of morality can have any meaning. It is only when such belief is restored to people's hearts that the present moral chaos has any chance of being resolved.

One thing, however, which even people who have belief in the Last Day tend to do, is to project the whole matter into the distant future. There is an *ayat* in *Surat al-A'raf* we mentioned earlier in which "*hanging heavy*" is a reference to the continual imminence of the Last Day and to the fact that just on the other side of the fragile fabric of the space-time dimension in which we live lies a vastly greater reality where time and space are governed by completely different laws than those which pertain here. Allah says in *Surat ar-Rum*, and there are many similar *ayats*:

> On the Day the Last Hour arrives the evildoers
>   will swear they have not even tarried for an hour.
>   That is the extent to which they are deceived. (30:54)

So it will appear when we arrive in the Next World that our time in this world was almost nothing.

One way of understanding this is to think about what happens when we wake from a dream. We may feel intensely alive and travel great distances and do many things in our dream world, and even seem to spend much time there, but when we wake up, the whole experience immediately fades into complete insubstantiality, leaving us with nothing more than a pleasant or unpleasant aftertaste depending on the nature of the dream. Our lives in this world will have the same quality for us when we arrive in the Next World as dreams have for us in this one when we wake in the morning. There is a saying of 'Ali which bears this out:

People are asleep and when they die they wake up.
(Al-'Ajaluni in Kashf al-Khafa)

The point is that this world is not really real at all in an absolute sense. It is always amusing to hear people say, "You should live in the real world," because the truth is that the world they are talking about is frequently less real than some people's dreams. We find in the Qur'an:

The life of the world is nothing
but a game and a diversion.
The abode of the Next World –
that is truly Life if they only knew. (29:64)

So true reality is what we experience after we die. This world is merely a shadow of what we will find on the other side of death. Allah says in *Surat al-Baqara* about some people in the Garden:

When they are given fruit there as provision,
they will say, 'This is what we were given before.'
But they were only given a simulation of it. (2:24)

In other words the things we have in this world are in fact a faint shadow of their true reality which we will only experience fully in the Next World, either as the blissful delights of the Garden or as the agonising terrors of the Fire. That is why these things are described in the Qur'an in such vivid and graphic detail. One example among many others can be found in *Surat al Kahf*:

We have made ready for the wrongdoers a Fire
whose billowing walls of smoke will hem them in.

If they call for help, they will be helped with water
like seething molten brass, frying their faces.
What a noxious drink! What an evil repose!
But as for those who believe and do right actions,
We will not let the wage of the good-doers go to waste.
They will have Gardens of Eden
with rivers flowing under them.
They will be adorned in them
with bracelets made of gold
and wear green garments
made of the finest silk and rich brocade,
reclining there on couches under canopies.
What an excellent reward! What a wonderful repose!

(18:29-31)

And do not make the mistake of thinking that these things are distant from us. As the Book and *Sunna* make clear we ourselves are moulding our own fates, minute by minute, hour by hour, and day by day and are only prevented from perceiving the reality of our actions by the thinnest of veils. We find in *Surat al-'Ankabut*:

They ask you to hasten the punishment
but Hell already encircles the unbelievers. (29:54)

When the Prophet ﷺ was performing the Eclipse Prayer with the Companions, he at one point reached his hand out towards the right and then withdrew it and at another leaned his whole body back and away from the left. When they asked him why he had done that, he said that first he had seen a bunch of grapes in the Garden and had wanted to reach out and pluck it to show people what was in store for them and then he had seen the Fire and had recoiled from the intensity of its heat. No, the other world is very close and very real.

One thing that really brought this home to me was something that happened while I was living in Atlanta at the end of the seventies. A woman who had recently entered Islam came and told me about a dream that her ten year-old daughter had had the previous night. The girl had seen herself with a lot of other people on a very high narrow bridge crossing over an immensely deep chasm of fire. She was finding it increasingly difficult to move and finally she toppled from it and found herself turning over and over falling towards the fire. When she looked up she could see people looking down at her from the bridge praying for help for her. Suddenly an angel swooped down, gathered her up, and she found herself back on the bridge. She woke up in quite a state and told her mother what she had seen.

I told the woman about the *Sirat* and the events of the Last Day but the significance of the dream did not finally hit home until almost ten years later when I was living again in England. The mother of the girl had kept in loose touch over the years and we received news that her daughter was soon to be married. We heard that what had happened was that in her early teens the girl had gone completely off the rails and totally rejected Islam and basically gone on the streets. But recently she had once more returned wholeheartedly to the *deen* and was going to marry a young Muslim man of very high reputation. The girl's dream of her crossing the narrow bridge, an event which only occurs on the Last Day, had truly prefigured the course of her life in this world. So it is evident that the events of the Next World really do mirror our lives in this one.

THE EVENTS OF THE LAST DAY

> *As for him who is given his Book in his right hand,*
> *he will say, 'Here, come and read my Book!*
> *I counted on meeting my Reckoning.'*
> *He will have a very pleasant life*
> *in an elevated Garden,*
> *its ripe fruit hanging close to hand.* (69:18-22)

> *But as for him who is given his Book in his left hand,*
> *he will say, 'If only I had not been given my Book*

and had not known about my Reckoning!
If only death had really been the end!
My wealth has been of no use to me.
My power has vanished.'
'Seize him and truss him up.
Then roast him in the Blazing Fire.' (69:24-30)

What is going to be presented now is a kind of sketch plan gleaned from the Book and *Sunna* of the events of the Last Day, with the caveat, of course, that what is being described takes place outside the space-time laws that govern us here and so cannot really be fixed in space-time terms. What is certain is that we will know exactly what these things are when we see them from the descriptions we have been given.

When someone dies they go first to the in-between world (*barzakh*) of the grave. There they will be questioned by the angels, Munkar and Nakir, who will ask them who their Lord was, what their *deen* was, and who their Messenger was. Some find themselves tongue-tied and unable to answer. When it is said to them: "How is it that you can't answer when we saw you praying and fasting with the Muslims?" they reply that they just said what people said and did what they did. According to a person's state the grave will either be spacious and pleasant with a window opening onto their promised place in the Garden or it will close in on them and crush them and they will be beaten by angels with iron bars and tormented in other ways and there will be a window in it opening onto their destined place in the Fire.

Israfil's final trumpet blast will call all human beings out from their graves and they will all be gathered together, every single human being from the beginning to the end of time, on a vast plain. It will be extremely hot there and some will literally be up to their necks in their own perspiration. We have a hadith from al-Miqdad 🙏 in which he said that he heard the Messenger of Allah 🕌 say: "On the Day of Rising the sun will come close to people until it seems about a mile above them and mankind will perspire according to their actions. The perspiration will reach up to the ankles of some, the knees of others, the waists of others, while for others it will reach up to the level of their mouths," and Allah's Messenger indicated his own mouth with his hand. (Muslim)

It will only be comparatively comfortable for those Allah gives shade to, among whom, according to a famous hadith, are: just rulers, those who spent their youth in worship, those whose hearts are attached to the mosque, people who love one another for the sake of Allah alone, those who do *dhikr* alone and weep, those who restrain themselves in the face of an open invitation to unlawful sex, and those who give secretly to the extent that their right hand does not know what their left hand has given.

While there, each person will be given their book, that detailed and intimate record of every moment of their life from which nothing whatsoever is omitted, that journal which is being written down moment by moment during our life in this world. As we saw in the *ayat* at the beginning, being given our book in the right hand will be a sign of success whereas getting it in the left hand or behind the back will be a sign of abysmal failure.

Then the *Mizan*, the Balance, is set up in which the actions recorded in our books are weighed and:

> *Those whose scales are heavy,*
> *they are the successful.*
> *Those whose scales are light,*
> *they are the losers of their selves,*
> *remaining in Hell timelessly, for ever.* (23:103-4)

In respect of this the Prophet ﷺ warned people to be careful to give to other people the rights which are due to them because if they do not, it is at this point that those others come to claim them. They take what is owed to them from the good actions in the balance of the person who owes something to them and transfer it to their own scale; and many will find their balances changing from heavy to light on account of this.

From here we set off across the *Sirat,* the narrow bridge so vividly pictured by the young girl in her dream. As we live in this world, so we will cross the *Sirat.* Those who spent their lives truly striving in the path of Allah and His Messenger 🕌 will cross like the wind. Some will cross running, others walking, others crawling on their hands and knees being snagged by their wrong actions which appear as sharp hooks which claw at them as they pass. There are others who fail to cross and fall into the river of fire below.

There is a hadith transmitted by Abu Dawud which refers to these three stages of the Day of Rising, which was related by 'A'isha 🕌 the wife of the Prophet 🕌. She tells us that once she thought about Hellfire and it made her begin to weep. When the Messenger of Allah 🕌 asked her why she was weeping she replied, "I was thinking about Hellfire and it made me weep. Will you remember your family on the Day of Rising?" The Messenger of Allah 🕌 responded, "There are three places where no one will remember anyone else: at the Balance until the person knows whether their scale is light or heavy; at the giving of the Book, when the command comes to take it and read it, until the person knows whether it will come to their right hand, or to their left hand behind their back; and at the *Sirat* when it is placed across Hellfire."

Those Muslims who cross come to the *hawd* (basin) of the Prophet 🕌 which is a huge reservoir fed by a river whose water is whiter than milk, sweeter than honey, colder than snow and sweeter smelling than musk. It is surrounded by beautiful cups and all those who drink from it will never thirst again. Some, however, will be driven away from it by angels and they are those who deviate from the *Sunna* of the Messenger of Allah 🕌. Once again we find the connection between this world and the Next. Drinking from the hand of the Prophet 🕌 on the Last Day depends on a person having truly absorbed and practised his *Sunna* here in this world.

There is a hadith about the Basin found in the collections of

Ahmad, at-Tirmidhi and Ibn Majah where Thawban reported the Prophet 🌺 as saying, "The width of my *hawd* is similar to the distance between Aden and Amman of al-Balqa'. Its water is whiter than milk and sweeter than honey and its cups are as numerous as the stars in the sky. Anyone who has one drink from it will never feel thirsty again. The first to come to it will be the poor emigrants (*Muhajirun*), those with dishevelled heads and soiled clothes who do not marry delicate women and do not have doors opened for them."

Then those whose self-chosen destiny is the Fire and its timeless, endless, unspeakably atrocious tortures are herded together in chains and driven away into it. We seek refuge with Allah from that. Those who have chosen the Garden for themselves by having belief in Allah and His Messengers and have followed the path set down by Allah and His Messengers will be conducted to their places in the Garden where they will be with those they love and have all they could possibly desire and even more. Then those among them who are chosen will be taken to the Lookout Point from which they will be permitted to gaze on the Face of Allah, before which even the greatest of the unparalleled delights of Paradise will pale into total insignificance.

This, then, is a brief outline of the Last Day and what happens on it. The question every person needs to ask is whether they have prepared themselves for it? Death could come to anyone at any moment. As far as each person's individual destiny is concerned, the Last Day is the day they leave this world, because at that moment all possibility of further action is cut off.

The Decree

to believe in the Decree...

*T*he keys of the Unseen are in His possession.
>No one knows them but Him.
>He knows everything in the land and sea.
No leaf falls without His knowing it.
There is no seed in the darkness of the earth,
>and nothing moist or dry
>which is not in a Clear Book. (6:60)

Say: 'Nothing can happen to us
>except what Allah has ordained for us.
>>He is Our Master.
>It is in Allah that the believers should put their trust.' (9:51)

If Allah afflicts you with harm,
>no one can remove it except Him.
If He desires good for you,
>no one can avert His favour.
He bestows it on whichever of His slaves He wills.
>He is Ever-Forgiving, Most Merciful. (10:107)

Belief in the Decree is unnecessarily considered a difficult aspect of Islamic doctrine. It has been the subject of much discussion over many centuries both inside and outside the Muslim community. The basic belief is really very simple: that everything which happens in existence is in the foreknowledge of Allah, the Creator of the universe and cannot occur in any other way than the way it does but, at the same time, this does not affect the fact that everyone is absolutely accountable for what they do. Over the ages people have tried to bring the whole philosophical discussion of free-will versus determinism into this but to do so is actually to misunderstand the nature of existence. The vast majority of Muslims have no trouble in resolving the apparent paradox involved and comprehending that Allah, may He be exalted, has absolute control of existence but that they are completely responsible for their actions.

Allah says in His Noble Book:

> *We sent it down on a blessed night;*
> *   We are constantly giving warning.*
> *During it every wise decree is specified*
> *   by a command from Our presence.*
> *We are constantly sending out*
> *   as a mercy from your Lord.*
> *He is the All-Hearing, the All-Knowing:*
> *   the Lord of the heavens and the earth*
> *and everything in between them,*
> *   if you are people with certainty.*
> *There is no god but Him –*
> *   He gives life and causes to die –*
> *your Lord and the Lord of your forefathers,*
> *   the previous peoples.* (44:2-7)

The blessed night mentioned in these *ayats* is taken by many Qur'anic commentators to refer to the night of 15th Sha'ban, a night which as we know is celebrated by many Muslims as the *Layla al-Bara'a*. The reason for this night being marked out in this way is because in the *ayat* Allah, exalted is He, tells us that it is the time when His decree is made specific, particularly with respect to people's life-spans. This is confirmed by a hadith narrated by Abu Ya'la in which 'A'isha ﴿ asked the Prophet ﷺ why he fasted so much in the month of Sha'ban and he replied,

"In this month Allah writes down the death of everyone who will die during the coming year and I would like my destiny to reach me while I am fasting." This hadith is a good introduction to a matter which as a general rule receives insufficient attention from the Muslims in spite of its great importance as one of the six pillars of *iman*: Belief in *al-Qadar* – the Divine Decree.

The Prophet ﷺ said about belief in the famous hadith from 'Umar ﷺ on which this book is based, that it is: "That you believe in Allah, His angels, His Books, His Messengers, and the Last Day and that you believe in the Decree, both its good and its evil." He added in some transmissions, "And both its sweet and its bitter." "Good" in this context is said to refer to obeying Allah and doing good, "evil" to wrong action and unbelief; "sweet" to things which human beings like, such as wealth and good health and all manifestations of Divine beauty, and "bitter" to things which human beings dislike, such as illness and poverty, abasement and all manifestations of Divine majesty.

Allah ﷻ makes the whole thing crystal clear for us in many *ayats* of His Book.

> The keys of the Unseen are in His possession.
>   No one knows them but Him.
> He knows everything in the land and sea.
>   No leaf falls without His knowing it.
> There is no seed in the darkness of the earth,
>   and nothing moist or dry
>   which is not in a Clear Book. (6:60)

There is nothing in existence other than what Allah has decided beforehand should be there.

> Nothing occurs, either in the earth or in yourselves,
>   without its being in a Book before We make it happen.
>   That is something easy for Allah (57:21)

Nothing whatsoever happens without the foreknowledge of Allah that it will take place.

Say: 'Nothing can happen to us
except what Allah has ordained for us.
He is Our Master.
It is in Allah that the believers
should put their trust.' (9:51)

This includes what happens, in detail, to every human being and the believer knows this and accepts it.

However, it happened so that Allah could settle
a matter whose result was preordained. (8:42)

Here Allah is referring to the predestination of a specific event: the victory at Badr.

Allah, exalted is He, is particularly specific in many *ayats* about the preordination of the time of death of every human being, saying for example in *Sura Ali 'Imran*:

No self can die except with Allah's permission,
at a predetermined time. (3:145)

And in *Sura Fatir*:

And no living thing lives long
or has its life cut short
without that being in a Book.
That is easy for Allah. (35:11)

The Prophet ﷺ was equally explicit on the subject of the Divine Decree and there are several hadiths which deal with it in a very overt way.

In the well-known hadith reported by 'Abdullah ibn Mas'ud which we find in both al-Bukhari and Muslim, he said ﷺ, "The creation of each of you takes place by being brought together in your mother's womb for forty days as a drop, then for a similar period as a clot, then for a similar period as a lump of flesh. Then the angel is sent to it to breathe the *ruh* into it and is ordered to dictate four things: its provision, its lifespan, its actions and whether it will be in the Fire or the Garden."

We can see from this hadith that the precise destiny of each individual is mapped out in detail before their emergence into this world.

In some advice he gave to his young cousin 'Abdullah ibn 'Abbas, the Prophet ﷺ said: "Know that whatever misses you could never have hit you and what hits you could never have missed you." (Ahmad, Abu Ya'la) At-Tirmidhi added in one transmission, "The pens have been lifted and the pages are dry." And in a similar vein he once said to Abu Hurayra ؓ, "The pen is dry with respect to what you will meet, Abu Hurayra." (Al-Bukhari, an-Nasa'i)

He said on another occasion ﷺ, "Everything is by a decree, even lack of strength and lack of intelligence." (Muslim, Ahmad)

The whole matter receives a classical formulation in the *Risala* of Ibn Abi Zayd al-Qayrawani:

> Everything that happens has been decreed by Allah, our Lord. The way things are decided is entirely in His hand and the way they happen is according to His Decree. He knows all things before they come into existence and they take place in the way He has already decided. There is nothing that His servants say or do which He has not decreed and does not have knowledge of. *"Does not He who creates know, when He is the Subtle and the All-Aware."* (67:14)
>
> He leads astray whoever He wills and in His justice debases them, and He guides whoever He wills and in His generosity grants them success. In that way everyone is eased by Him to what He already has knowledge of and has previously decreed, as to whether they are to be among the fortunate or the miserable.
>
> He is exalted above there being anything He does not desire in His kingdom, or that there should be anything not dependent on Him, or that there should be any creator of anything other than Him, the Lord of all people, the Lord of their actions, the One who decrees their

movements and the time of their death.

This is the way existence works, the way things are, and anyone who denies it or doubts it is a disbeliever by consensus. Anyone who believes it through knowledge but then does not accept it when it actually happens, is a *fasiq* – a deviant – by consensus.

Allah, exalted is He, says:

> *...that man will have nothing but what he strives for;*
> *that his striving will most certainly be seen;*
> *that he will then receive repayment of the fullest kind.*
>
> (53:38-40)

> *As for anyone who desires this fleeting existence,*
> *We hasten in it whatever We will*
> *to whoever We want.*
> *Then We will consign him to Hell*
> *where he will roast, reviled and driven out.*
> *But as for anyone who desires the Next World,*
> *and strives for it with the striving it deserves,*
> *being a believer,*
> *the striving of such people*
> *will be gratefully acknowledged.* (17:18-19)

Up to now we have only looked at the immutable nature of the Divine Decree and have yet to mention its corollary: human accountability and responsibility. From the beginning there have been people who have been puzzled by the apparent paradox between the predetermination of all actions and subsequent human responsibility for them. Some Companions even went to the Prophet 🕌 and asked him, "Messenger of Allah, then what is action for?" The Prophet 🕌 responded to them by saying, "Act. Each person is eased to that for which he was created." ('Abdullah ibn Ahmad ibn Hanbal and at-Tabarani in *al-Kabir*)

In another account narrated in the *Musnad* of Imam Ahmad, and in the works of al-Bukhari, Abu Dawud, at-Tirmidhi and Ibn Majah, the Prophet 🕌 added, "If he is one of the people of happiness, the actions of the people of happiness are made easy for him. If he is one of people of wretchedness, the actions of the people of wretchedness are made easy for him." Then he recited, *"As for him who gives out and has taqwa and confirms the Good, We will pave his way to Ease. But as for him who is stingy and self-satisfied, and denies the Good, We will pave his way to Difficulty."* (92:5-10)

This in fact makes the whole matter absolutely clear but some people have still tended to go wrong about it. There are two principle deviant positions which people take. On the one hand some claim that human beings have absolute freedom of will where action is concerned whereas on the other some claim the opposite and say that people are absolutely constrained and have no freedom whatsoever. These two deviations had their very early proponents and stories are told of how 'Ali and 'Umar ﷺ dealt with each of them.

'Ali ﷺ was confronted by one of the advocates of absolute free will who declared to him that he could by his own will decide to do whatever he liked. 'Ali said to him, "All right then, lift up your right arm." The man did so. "Now lift up your right leg." He did that. "Now your left arm." So the man was standing with both arms and one leg raised. "Now," said 'Ali, "raise the other leg!" And, of course, he couldn't and it remained firmly on the ground. By this simple expedient 'Ali demonstrated that the human will is necessarily constrained by many laws outside human control.

In the time of 'Umar ﷺ a small group of men who espoused the other deviant position, that all action was pointless, decided to go and spend all their time in a mosque and have their families bring them their meals and look after their needs. They called themselves "the *Mutawakkilun*" – those who put their trust in Allah. 'Umar ﷺ heard about them and went to visit them. After speaking to them he told them, "You are not *mutawakkilun* you are *muta'akilun* – people who expect others to feed them! Get out of the mosque and do something useful with your lives."

No, the truth is, as the Prophet ﷺ made clear to those Companions who came to him, where people are concerned, the Divine Decree is inextricably bound up with their actions, their destiny is inseparable from what they do. The hadith in al-Bukhari about the creation of the human being in the womb, the first half of which was quoted earlier, ends by the Prophet ﷺ saying, "By Allah, apart from Whom there is no other god, one of you will do the actions of the people of the Garden until there is nothing but an armspan between him and it and then what is written will supersede and he will do the actions of the people of the Fire and so enter it. And another of you will do the actions of the people of the Fire until there is nothing but an armspan between him and it and then what is written will supersede and he will do the actions of the people of the Garden and so enter it."

An illuminating example of how action and the Divine Decree are intertwined can be seen in something which happened on the day of Badr. Having set the battle in motion, the Prophet ﷺ retired with Abu Bakr ؓ to a straw hut which had been constructed for him at the edge of the battlefield. Once there, he raised his arms and began to call on Allah with great earnestness. Among the things he said ﷺ were the words, "O Allah give us the victory you have promised me. If You let this group of men perish today, You will no longer be worshipped on the earth." In his state of intense entreaty his cloak fell from him and Abu Bakr ؓ picked it up and put it back round his shoulders, saying to him, "Messenger of Allah, there is no need for this. Allah will certainly fulfil His promise to you." (Ibn Hisham) It was almost as if, out of his concern for him, Abu Bakr was suggesting that the Prophet ﷺ was somehow doubting the Divine Decree. But the Prophet ﷺ continued his calling on Allah until the tears were flowing freely down his cheeks. We know from the *ayat* quoted earlier, that the result of the battle was a foregone conclusion and certainly no human being before or since had greater knowledge of his Lord than the Prophet ﷺ. No, the truth is, that by his action of earnest entreaty to Allah, the Prophet ﷺ far from doubting the Divine Decree, was in fact actively participating in it.

So from one point of view we are in fact, day by day, forging our own destiny through the actions we make. We are continually faced by different situations and different possibilities of action and we make our decisions according to what we think best at the time. The result of those decisions is written down by the two angels responsible for recording our actions and that record, containing our ultimate destiny, will be handed to us on the Day of Rising. On that Day we will know for certain that we have no one to blame for what we find there but ourselves and that Allah is absolutely just with His slaves. That is our reality.

> *We have fastened the destiny of every man about his neck*
> *and on the Day of Rising We will bring out a Book for him*
> *which he will find spread open in front of him.*
> *'Read your Book! Today your own self*
> *is reckoner enough against you!'* (17:13-14)

We are responsible and accountable for what we do. We must leave the reality of overall Lordship to Allah to Whom it alone belongs. He says of Himself:

> *Certainly it is to Us they will return.*
> *Then their Reckoning is Our concern.* (88:25-26)

And furthermore:

> *He will not be questioned about what He does,*
> *but they will be questioned.* (21:23)

This is why we find that the Prophet ﷺ in spite of his incomparable status as the beloved of Allah and his knowledge that he had Allah's complete forgiveness for any possible failing, was ceaselessly active in seeking the pleasure of His Lord until the time he died. And the same applies to all those who have followed him inwardly and outwardly, the Rightly Guided Caliphs, the great Companions, and the *awliya'* and the right-acting Muslims of the community through all the generations down to our own time. Of all people they have had the greatest knowledge of, and the deepest belief in, the Divine Decree and at the same time have had the most reason to be confident of the mercy of Allah. Yet without exception they have rejected any hint of complacency, have been scrupulous in avoiding what is displeasing to Allah, and throughout their lives have tirelessly sought out those actions which will make them pleasing to their Lord. This is the form that profound understanding of the nature of the Divine Decree inevitably takes.

A greater elaboration of this matter is to be found in a treatise written by the eminent nineteenth-century Moroccan scholar Ahmad ibn 'Ajiba, part of which is included here.

> As for evidence for the Decree in His Mighty Book, Allah says, "*We have created all things in due measure.*" (54:49) meaning brought them forth by a prior decree. Allah ﷻ says, "*We have listed everything in a clear register*" (36:12), referring to the Preserved Tablet on which every existent thing is inscribed. Allah says, "*Everything has its measure with Him*" (13:8) and, "*Allah's command is a preordained decree*" (33:38) and, "*So that Allah could settle a matter whose result was preordained*" (8:42). Allah ﷻ further says, "*Nothing occurs, either in the earth or in yourselves, without its being in a Book before We make it happen. That is something easy for Allah.*" (57:22) And, "*Nothing happens, either on the earth*" – such as droughts, famines, earthquakes and floods – "*or in yourselves*" – such as illness and death – "*without its being in a Book*" – the Preserved Tablet – "*before We make it happen.*" (57:21)
>
> Following on from this Allah ﷻ says, "*That is so that you will not be grieved about the things that pass you by*" – because it was foreordained from pre-eternity that they would not come about or would not continue, so you should not be sad about something which you were never going to have in the first place – "*or exult about the things that come to you*"

(57:23), because even before it appeared it was destined for you and bound to come to you. What is desired is a balanced attitude towards withholding and giving, contraction and expansion, loss and gain, abasement and might, poverty and wealth, health and illness, and other different states, because all these things occur according to preordained decrees. So do not be excessively sad about anything which you do not have or be overjoyed about anything that comes to you.

Allah ﷻ says, "*Allah has appointed a measure for all things.*" (65:3), meaning a known lifespan and predetermined time of occurrence, which cannot be brought forward or delayed by a single instant. Allah ﷻ says about the time of death, "*No self can die except with Allah's permission, at a predetermined time,*" (3:145) meaning that a person's death is determined before they are even born. Allah ﷻ says, "*It is He who created you from clay and then decreed a fixed term, and another fixed term is specified with Him.*" (6:2) The first refers to death and the second to the Rising from the dead.

Allah ﷻ says, "*It is He who takes you back to Himself at night, while knowing the things you perpetrate by day, and then wakes you up again, so that a specified term may be fulfilled*" (6:60), so that you may be certain that the end of your term was determined by Allah before time. He says, "*Then when death comes to one of you, Our messengers take him, and they do not fail in their task,*" (6:61), in other words they come at exactly the right time, neither a minute early or late.

Allah ﷻ says, "*Every nation has an appointed time. When their appointed time comes, they cannot delay it a single hour or bring it forward.*" (10:49) Allah ﷻ says, "*And no living thing lives long or has its life cut short without that being in a Book.*" (35:11) The meaning of the *ayat* is that no one is given a long life or a short one without that being preordained and recorded in the Preserved Tablet. It is said that a decrease in lifespan is in the knowledge of the angels but when someone maintains ties of kinship, for instance, the increase which is with Allah appears. The slave has only one life with Allah which can neither be increased nor decreased.

As for His words, *"Allah erases whatever He wills or endorses it,"* (13:39), it means: He obliterates what is with the angels and confirms what is with Him, which is the Mother of the Book. Allah ﷻ says, *"Though some of you may die before that time – so that you may reach a predetermined age and so that hopefully you will use your intellect. It is He who gives life and causes to die."* (40:67-68) This means that some people die before becoming old whereas the time of others may be deferred so that they reach a stated term which was already known before time. The angels record that term when the spirit is breathed into a person in the womb.

Hopefully you will understand and recognise that both death and life are in the hand of Allah and, therefore, that no cause, be it the plague or anything else, has any real effect in terms of bringing about death. Rather the entire affair belongs to Allah. That is why He said, *"It is He who gives life and causes to die,"* (40:68) He alone does these things, nothing else. *"When He decides on something"* – death or anything else – *"He just says to it, 'Be!' and it is."* (19:35) He says, *"When Allah's time comes it cannot be deferred, if you only knew."* (71:4) These *ayats* demonstrate how the length of a person's life is clearly defined. All lifespans were determined in pre-eternity. Allah does not delay nor bring forward anyone's time of death, either by the plague or anything else. So people should be calm in the face of the Decree and wait to see what Allah will do with them.

As for evidence in the *Sunna*, the Prophet ﷺ said to Ibn 'Abbas, "Ibn 'Abbas, I will teach you some words. Be careful regarding Allah and He will take care of you. Be careful regarding Allah and you will find Him in front of you. Recognise Allah in ease and He will recognise you

The Natural Form of Man

in hardship. Know that whatever misses you could never have hit you and what hits you could never have missed you." (Ahmad) He added in another transmission, "The pens have been lifted and the pages are dry," (At-Tirmidhi) indicating that what misses someone because it was not written for them will never reach them, be it good or evil, life or death. The Prophet ﷺ said to Abu Hurayra ؓ "The pen is dry with respect to what you will meet, Abu Hurayra." (Al-Bukhari, an-Nasa'i)

The Prophet ﷺ said, "Everything is by a decree, even lack of power and cleverness." Malik transmitted it in the *Muwatta'*. The Prophet ﷺ said, "A man can do the actions of someone destined for the Garden until there is only an armspan between him and it, and then what is written will overtake him and he will do the actions of someone destined for the Fire and enter it. A man can do the actions of someone destined for the Fire until there is only an armspan between him and it, and then what is written will overtake him and he will do the actions of someone destined for the Garden and enter it." Al-Bukhari and others related it.

The Prophet ﷺ said, "Provision seeks out a man as his term seeks him." (Al-Bazzar, at-Tabarani, Ibn 'Adi) The Prophet ﷺ said, "Allah entrusts an angel to the womb who says, 'O Lord, a drop! O Lord, a clot! O Lord, a piece of flesh!' When the *ruh* is breathed into it, he says, 'O Lord, what is its provision? What is its life-span? Wretched or happy?' All of that is decreed in his mother's womb," as the Prophet ﷺ said in what al-Bukhari and Muslim related.

The Prophet ﷺ said in explaining the reality of belief: "It is that you believe in Allah, his angels, His Books, His Messengers, and the Last Day and that you believe in the Decree, both its good and its bad." He added in some transmissions, "Both its sweet and its bitter." The "good" of the decree refers to obedience to Allah and doing good.

The "bad" is unbelief. The "sweet" are things which are in harmony with the human being, like wealth and health and all types of beauty. The "bitter" is what pains a human being, like illness and poverty, abasement and all types of majesty. All of that has already been decreed and decided.

Anyone who doubts this is an unbeliever by consensus. Anyone who believes in the Decree in terms of knowledge, but is not content with it when it actually occurs, is a deviant by consensus. That is why Malik ﷺ said, "Whoever has the *Shari'a* without *tasawwuf* deviates." Shaykh Abu'l-Hasan ﷺ said, "Whoever does not breathe his final breath knowing this knowledge of ours (*tasawwuf*), dies persisting in great wrong actions without being aware of it." Whoever does not admire the people of purity does not desire to be described with purity. Purity is contentment and submission to all that emerges from the All-Wise, All-Knowing.

The Prophet ﷺ said, "The Spirit of Purity conveyed to my spirit: 'A soul will not die until it has received its full provision, so fear Allah and be temperate in seeking it.'" The Prophet ﷺ said, "Your Lord has decreed four things: physique and character, provision and lifespan." At-Tabarani related this in *al-Awsat*. In the transmission of Ahmad we find, "Allah ﷻ has decreed five things for each slave: his lifespan, his provision, his steps, where he will die, whether he will be wretched or happy." What is meant by steps are the steps which he will walk.

So provision, both physical and spiritual, was allotted before time, just as lifespans and steps are allotted. It is the same with ranks and stations. The Pen has dried having written all of that. The Companions said, "Messenger of Allah, then what is action for?" The Prophet ﷺ said, "Act. Each is eased to that which was created for him." ('Abdullah ibn Ahmad ibn Hanbal, at-Tabarani in al-Kabir) [In another narration he added],

"If he is one of the people of happiness, the actions of the people of happiness are made easy for him. If he is one of people of wretchedness, the actions of the people of wretchedness are made easy for him." Then he recited, *"As for him who gives out and is godfearing and confirms the Good, We will pave his way to Ease. But as for him who is stingy and self-satisfied, and denies the Good, We will pave his way to Difficulty."* (92:5-10) (Ahmad, al-Bukhari, Abu Dawud, at-Tirmidhi, Ibn Majah)

If you were to ask, "If the Decree has already preceded determining what will be, so the slave cannot avoid it, for what reason is the slave called to account and punished?" the answer is that by Allah's radiant wisdom manifest in human beings, He made them accountable according to whether they intend good or evil by what they do. In reality, they are pulled by a chain but the *Shari'a* ascribes their actions to them because of that accountability and so the proof against them is established. Allah ﷻ says, *"Say: 'Allah's is the conclusive argument. If He had willed He could have guided every one of you.'"* (6:149) So the kingdom is His kingdom and the slaves are His slaves. *"He will not be questioned about what He does, but they will be questioned."* (21:23)

It is the same with provision. It is allotted before-time and guaranteed by the surety of Allah ﷻ but His wisdom demands that the secrets of Lordship be concealed and, therefore, it is accompanied by the existence of the means but is not brought about by them. So the means must exist but the absence of them in reality must be acknowledged. Yes, whoever is truly godfearing and devotes himself to Allah is provided for without any cause. The Almighty says, *"Whoever has taqwa of Allah – He will give him a way out and provide for him from where he does not expect. Whoever puts his trust in Allah – He will be enough for him."* (65:3) Shaykh Abu'l-Abbas said, "People have means, but our means are faith and *tawqa*." Then he recited, "*If only the people of the cities had believed and been godfearing, We would have opened up to them blessings from heaven and earth.*" (7:96)

As for the words of the right-acting first generations about the Decree, among their well-known sayings is, "Whatever Allah wills will be. Whatever our Lord did not will, will not be." It is also said that this is a hadith. 'Umar ibn 'Abdu'l-'Aziz said, "I have no happiness except in the place of the Decree." One of them was asked, "What do you want?" He answered, "Whatever Allah decrees." Ibn 'Ata'illah said in the *Hikam*. "Every breath you breathe emerges according to a preordained decree." He also said, "How can your subsequent asking be a cause of His prior giving? The decree from Before-time is too majestic to be ascribed to any action. His concern for you did not come from you. Where were you when He directed His concern to you and faced you with His guardianship? There is no sincerity of action in pre-eternity. No state exists in pre-eternity. There was only pure overflowing favour and immense giving." He means that what was decreed for you in the World of the Unseen before time is what appears for you in the visible world. There was no possibility of action in that time by which you could have deserved a gift nor of any state by which you could have deserved being brought close to Allah or reaching Him. His giving to you is only a gracious favour from Him and generosity. Allah possesses immense favour.

Know that people fall into four categories regarding their view of the Decree. The first look at the prior decree and its attached judgement. The second look at ends since they know that actions are by their seals. The third look at the moment and are not distracted either by what has come before or the ends, only performing what they are obliged to do in the moment, knowing that 'the *faqir* is the child of the moment.' They only see the moment which they are in. The fourth see Allah alone since they know that the past, future and present are turned about in the Hand of the Real and are disposed by His rulings. All moments accept change and the state can change. They witness everything as being in His hand. This category have rest from the turbidity of management since their witnessing the Manager makes them absent from prior decree, which is different from the first three who are dominated by witnessing separation.

The first group is distracted by fear of prior decrees. The second is dazzled by fear of ends and seals. By seeing the rule of the moment and witnessing its rulings, the third is made absent to witnessing the Maker of the Moment. When the veil is removed from the fourth category, and they witness the Lord of Lords, witnessing the One distracts them from everything but nothing distracts them from Allah. That is why it is said, "The realised man is the one who does not see other-than-Allah in either Abode and does not witness other-than-Allah with Allah. Everything is subjected to him and he is not subjected to anything. By it he is pure from the turbidity of everything and his purity is not disturbed by anything. The One distracts him from everything and nothing distracts him from the One."

In short, the one who wants constant tranquillity should throw himself down before Allah, look in every moment at what emerges from Allah, and be content under the courses of what is decreed for him and so withdraw from his management and choice. Reflect on what the Qutb Sidi Yaqut al-'Arshi said:

There is only what He wills,
  so leave your concerns and prostrate.
Leave everything which distracts you from Him
  and let it go.

So it is clear that everything that has occurred or will occur was decreed in pre-eternity and the moment and mode of its occurrence are specified and cannot be advanced or delayed. It is, however, part of the wisdom of the All-Wise that He has covered this secret with the cloak of wisdom, and given everything a cause. So the Decree descends in its moment which was singled out for it before time and it is concealed in the existence of its cause and so it is said, "So-and-so did that," and "This happened to him" and "So-and-so went to a place where there was plague and died from it," or "He carried it to another place." Stopping at this outward appearance without looking into the inward aspect of it and the way the Decree emerges is a dense veil and crass ignorance. It may even lead to unbelief if someone believes in cause and effect and denies the Decree. Many feet slip up regarding this matter among those who lay claim to knowledge. Such people only have the formulae of knowledge not its reality.

Certainty about the Decree is strengthened by reports which came with multiple transmissions about matters before they occurred which then came about. Some came by way of Revelation, like the words of Allah ﷻ, *"Allah has promised those of you who believe and do right actions that He will make them successors in the land as He made those before them successors."* (24:55) Then Allah established the Companions firmly in the East and the West. Another example can be found in the words of Allah ﷻ, *"Alif Lam Mim. The Romans have been defeated in the land nearby, but after their defeat they will themselves be victorious in a few years' time."* (30:14) Then they defeated Persia at the time of Hudaybiyya. Allah says, *"You will enter the Masjid al-Haram in safety, Allah willing, shaving your heads and cutting your hair without any fear."* (48:27) That occurred on the Day of the Opening [of Makka to Islam].

As for the Prophet ﷺ reporting about unseen future

things, there are innumerable instances of that. The Prophet ﷺ warned about the seditions which would occur after him as if he was actually seeing them. All of those things occurred. If everything occurred by chance as the Rafidites and Qadarites say, then there could not be reports of things which had not yet happened which then occurred. If you say, "All you have done is to report something well known since all the Muslims say this," I said, "Our intention is not confined to mere knowledge. We want to inculcate certainty. There is no doubt that that is what is desired. It is one of the armies of lights and it leads to success. Allah is the Guide to the Straight Path."

This magnificent and luminous passage must not be understood merely as theology, for it emerges from the lived experience of people who witnessed at each instant the truth of the Decree.

Ihsan

is to worship Allah as if
you see Him, for if you do
not see Him, He sees you.

Ihsan

is to worship Allah as if you see Him...
for if you do not see Him He sees you

*A*llah has acted graciously to us.
As for those who fear Allah and are steadfast,
Allah does not allow to go to waste
the wage of any people who do good. (12:90)

Those who do good will have the best and more! (10:26)

In the *ayats* above, the phrase '*do good*' derives from the Arabic term *ihsan*, and this further element known as *ihsan* is absolutely indispensable to the activation of the outward practices and inner beliefs we have been examining. You may have a car which is mechanically in perfect working order and whose fuel tank and reservoirs are full of all the right fluids to ensure it will run smoothly but unless you turn the key in the ignition and create the spark which sets the whole thing in motion you are not going anywhere. *Ihsan* is that vital inner dynamic needed to bring to life the whole pattern of practices and beliefs which make up the body of Islam for every Muslim.

The Arabic word *ihsan* comes from the verb *ahsana* which means to do good, to act well, to do something expertly, to master something, but although these meanings are indeed included in it, the word as it is used in this context comes, as we have seen, from the well-known saying of the Prophet Muhammad ﷺ which forms the basis of this book in which he was asked to define the *deen* or life-practice he was sent to convey to mankind. As is clear from his definition of it – *Ihsan* is to worship Allah as if you see

Him, for if you do not see Him, He sees you – the quality of *ihsan* is at base awareness of the omnipresence of Allah and the only faculty capable of perceiving this is the human heart. For this reason the people of knowledge have said that the development of *ihsan* within the individual Muslim involves the purification of their heart and this process of purification has traditionally been given the name of *tasawwuf* or sufism.

Many Muslims consider that simply by performing the actions outlined by the five pillars: by doing the five prayers, paying *zakat*, fasting Ramadan and going on *Hajj*, that by doing these things alone they are fulfilling the purpose for which Allah has created them. However, the Prophet ﷺ makes it clear to us in several ways that the action on its own is not what is demanded of us. The actions of the *deen* are, of course, indispensable; without them nothing is possible. It is, however, entirely possible to perform all the actions of the *deen* without them having any real effect whatsoever, without them really being worship of Allah at all.

Allah, exalted is He, says in the Qur'an about such actions that they are like ashes blown by the wind on a stormy day. Shaykh Ibn Ata'illah al-Iskandari says in his *Hikam*: "Actions are merely propped-up shapes. Their life-breath is the presence of the secret of sincerity in them." So without this dimension of sincerity – in Arabic *ikhlas* – no action has any weight, no action has a real on-going existence, no action will be recorded for us with Allah. The true nature of *ikhlas* is made clear for us in the Qur'anic *sura* which bears its name:

Say: He is Allah, Absolute Oneness.
Allah the Everlasting Sustainer of all.
He has not given birth and was not born.
And no one is comparable to Him. (112)

When you examine *Surat al-Ikhlas* you find that there is nothing mentioned in it except Allah, may He be exalted. This shows us that an action can only be called truly sincere if it is done for Allah alone. The way that this element of pure sincerity enters into an action is through the intention brought to it, as the Prophet ﷺ made clear in a famous hadith:

> The Amir al-Mu'minin, Abu Hafs 'Umar ibn al-Khattab said, "I heard the Messenger of Allah ﷺ say, 'Actions only go by intentions. Everyone gets what they intend. Anyone, therefore, who emigrates to Allah and His Messenger, his emigration is indeed to Allah and His Messenger. But anyone who emigrates to gain something of this world or to marry a woman, his emigration is to that to which he emigrated.'" (Al-Bukhari and Muslim)

The importance of this hadith is shown by the fact that many of the great scholars of hadith, including Imam al-Bukhari, started their collections with it. The *fuqaha* (jurisprudents) are agreed that the place where the intention must be made is the heart. It is not sufficient for it to be on the tongue alone. So the hadith makes it clear that the result of a person's action depends on what is in their heart, in other words on what they really want and expect from what they are doing.

This is not an easy thing; the heart frequently contains many conflicting motives and desires. You cannot just say you are doing something for the sake of Allah when the truth is that your motivation is ambivalent and confused. In order for an action to be truly for the sake of Allah and His Messenger ﷺ, your heart must be free of all the other conflicting emotions and desires which preoccupy most of us most of the time. In other words a pure intention demands a purified heart. Since, as we have seen, for an action to count, it must be preceded and accompanied by a pure intention, it follows that a purified heart is necessary in order for our worship of Allah to be effective, in order to achieve the purpose for which we have been put here by our Lord.

In the seminal hadith which has formed the basis of this book in which the angel Jibril ﷺ came and sat with the Prophet ﷺ with the object of making clear to the Companions and to all subsequent generations of Muslims the nature of their *deen*, it is divided into three complementary parts: Islam, which is defined in terms of the actions represented by the five pillars – affirming the two aspects of witnessing to the Divine unity and the Messengership of Muhammad, may Allah bless him and grant him peace (*shahadatayn*), establishing the prayer, paying *zakat*, fasting Ramadan, and going on *Hajj*; *Iman*, the belief structure or inner landscape of every Muslim, which is defined as belief in Allah, the angels, the divinely revealed Books, the Prophets and Messengers of Allah, the Last Day and the Decree; and a third element, *Ihsan*, which is defined as being to worship Allah as if you see Him, for if you do not see Him, He sees you.

This third element of *ihsan*, directly tied in the hadith to the worship of Allah, to the practical implementation of the other two elements, implies an active and constant awareness of the presence of Allah. This, of course, requires a heart which has gone through a process of purification, a heart from which the worldly preoccupations which normally prevent us from being aware of the Divine Presence have been eliminated. This makes the purification of the heart an integral and necessary part of the *deen*. It is, however, vital to remember that while the actions of the *deen* need the element of *ihsan* to bring them to life, *ihsan* equally needs the actions of the *deen* in order to exist; they are interdependent and cannot be divorced from one another. Since the very early days of Islam, this science of the purification of the heart has been given the name of *tasawwuf*. The great fourteenth-century Moroccan scholar Shaykh Ahmad Zarruq who is known as much and more for his orthodox knowledge of Islamic law as for his inward knowledge, and who is buried in Libya, said in this context:

> The position of *tasawwuf* with respect to the *deen* is like that of the spirit with respect to the body because it is synonymous with *ihsan* which is, as the Messenger of Allah ﷺ explained to Jibril, "to worship Allah as if you see Him"

and integral to the *deen* as a whole. Aspects of *tasawwuf* which have been defined, delineated and explained amount to about two thousand but all of them are merely facets of one thing: a person's sincerity in turning to Allah, mighty is He and majestic, and Allah knows best.

There are great differences in the way different gnostics have described the one Reality and that indicates the difficulty of grasping it in its entirety. The expression of each person is according to what he has understood of it. Everything that is said is about its details, and the view of each person, is according to his station with respect to knowledge, action, state, tasting and other things. That is the source of the disagreements about the nature of *tasawwuf.*

That is why in his book *Hilya* about great Muslim scholars and sufis of the past, when Abu Nu'aym, may Allah have mercy on him, deals with each person, he adds one of the sayings which is appropriate to the state of that person. The point is that everyone with a portion of sincere turning to Allah has a share of *tasawwuf,* and that the *tasawwuf* of every sufi consists in the sincerity of their turning to Allah, so understand that.

A condition for sincere turning to Allah is, however, that it is done in a way which is pleasing to Allah, mighty is He and majestic, and it is not valid without that condition being fulfilled, for '*He is not pleased with ingratitude in His slaves.*' (38:7) So true faith is necessary and acting by the norms of Islam is absolutely essential. There can be no *tasawwuf* except through an understanding of Islamic law because the outward judgements of Allah, mighty is He and majestic, can only be known through it. In the same way Islamic law has no meaning without *tasawwuf* because the validity of actions is dependent on the intention brought to them, which in turn entails sincere turning to Allah.

Therefore Islamic law and *tasawwuf* must be combined since they are inextricably bound together, just as spirits are joined to bodies. Bodies are the necessary vehicles for the spirits, just as bodies are only brought to life by the existence of the spirits within them. All this is encapsulated by the famous saying of Imam Malik ibn Anas: "Anyone who espouses *tasawwuf* without applying Islamic law is a heretic. Anyone who applies Islamic law without espousing *tasawwuf* is a deviant. Whoever combines the two achieves realisation."

Imam al-Ghazali, may Allah cover him with mercy, gives *ihsan*, the science of *tasawwuf*, the legal status of being *fard 'ayn*, an individual obligation for every Muslim, on the basis that, apart from the Prophets and Messengers of Allah, there is no human being whose heart is not in need of purification, making it clear that it is something which must be undertaken by all Muslims. This is because people with hearts full of impurities are bound to associate other things with Allah in their worship of Him and it is clear from many *ayats* and hadiths that associating other things with Allah is among the worst of wrong actions, even if it is done unconsciously. So the necessary task is to purify the heart but what is the nature of the impurities which need to be removed from it? The people of Allah have listed the things which clog up the human heart under five headings: the experiencing self (*nafs*), Satan (*Shaytan*), the physical appetites (*shahawat*), the subtle desires (*hawa*), and love of this world (*hubb ad-dunya*). We should look briefly at each of these in turn in order to see exactly what is involved.

THE NAFS

In the introduction to this book there was an examination of how every human being acquires their own unique identity. This identity or self-form is known in Arabic as the *nafs*. We saw how this individual identity, made up of many contributory factors, is built up over time, starting at the moment of birth. Everyone has certain determined genetic elements which preordain their physical form and basic temperamental characteristics and these combine with the many varied experiences which make up their early lives, leading every individual to adopt a more or less fixed picture of themselves. This self-picture, this acquired identity, from then on becomes the "me" through which every individual interfaces with the world. This "self" is far less fixed than most of us think and is in reality fluid and open to radical transformation, given the circumstances which make that transformation possible, and we will return to that a little later. At the same time it is how we actually experience ourselves at any given moment and therefore the locus within which all the various obstacles listed above, which prevent us from having an unobscured view of how things really are, have their effect and for that reason, because it is the seat of all the others, it is the first on the list.

SHAYTAN

Next comes Satan – in Arabic *Shaytan* whose plural in Arabic is *shayateen* or in English *shaytans*. Sometimes the singular – *Shaytan* – is used synonymously for Iblis, the first of the *shaytans*. The first thing to do is to put aside nearly all the mythical lore about the devil with which many of us have been bombarded for most of our lives. For most people of this time *Satan* represents a kind of absolute evil force which is in a perpetual battle with God representing absolute good, in a sort of good-versus-evil Star Wars scenario in which it is never quite certain who the final victor is going to be. On the other hand it is quite certain that *shaytans* do exist and are experienced in very real terms as malevolent and negative influences in people's lives.

The truth, however, is that the *shaytans* are merely creatures among all the others Allah has created and have no power whatsoever in the face of the Divine Omnipotence. They have merely been given by Allah a very limited power to misguide those human beings who allow themselves to be misled by them from the safe path of Divine guidance which has been communicated at the hands and on the tongues of the Prophets and Messengers of Allah throughout human history. There are various complementary passages in the Qur'an speaking about *Shaytan* – who also has the name Iblis in Arabic – and saying how he came to take on the role in existence he occupies. One representative passage is found in *Surat al-A'raf*:

> *We created you and then formed you*
>   *and then We said to the angels,*
>   *"Prostrate to Adam,"*
> *and they prostrated – except for Iblis.*
>   *He was not among the prostrators.*
> *He said, "What prevented you from prostrating*
>   *when I commanded you to?"*
> *He replied, "I am better than him.*
>   *You created me from fire*
>   *and You created him from clay."*
> *He said, "Descend from Heaven.*
>   *It is not for you to be arrogant in it.*
>   *So get out!*
>   *You are one of the abased."*
> *He said, "Grant me a reprieve*
>   *until the day they are raised up."*
> *He said, "You are one of the reprieved."*
> *He said, "By Your misguidance of me,*
>   *I will lie in ambush for them*
>   *on Your Straight Path.*
>   *Then I will come at them,*
>   *from in front of them and behind them,*
>   *from their right and from their left.*
>   *You will not find most of them thankful."*
> *He said, "Get out of it,*
>   *reviled and driven out.*
>   *As for those of them who follow you,*
>   *I will fill up Hell*
>   *with every one of you."* (7:10-17)

Satan has no direct power over human beings whatsoever, in other words he cannot make anyone do anything. His power is limited to that of suggestion; he can only provoke evil impulses and goad people on to do evil actions and they can either resist or obey. The question is how can people recognise these impulses when they arrive so that they can be on their guard against them and avoid going down the road Satan is trying to persuade them into taking?

The great ninth-century scholar and sufi Abu'l-Qasim al-Junayd wrote a treatise on correct conduct in which he delineates three kinds of inner impulses to which human beings are subject: angelic impulses which come when Allah wishes to assist someone to do good; impulses from the self prompted by the lower appetites and desire for comfort; and satanic impulses originating in the suggestions of Satan. It is obviously vitally important to be able to distinguish between these impulses so that the person concerned will be able to avoid self-destructive actions and choose those which will produce a fruitful outcome.

The sign that an impulse is angelic in origin is firstly that it will definitely accord with the Book and *Sunna* and secondly that it will arrive quietly and you will generally be reluctant to act on it, that it is not long lasting and is easily extinguished. If acted upon, however, it becomes stronger and stronger and easier and easier to fulfil and will leave the person who follows it up with a feeling of well-being and certain knowledge that they have acted rightly.

The sign that an impulse has come from the self is that it almost always involves a degree of self-deception by which you persuade yourself to decrease in right action or increase in acts of self-indulgence often for the best possible reasons! A second sign is that this kind of impulse will usually be very persistent and come back and back in spite of all attempts to drive it away, like an infant whose desire for something is increased when they are denied it.

The sign that an impulse has a *shaytanic* source is that it will take advantage of any open doors to the lower appetites and desires and goad the person on to immediate self-gratification. It arrives all of a sudden as if out of nowhere and with great force, so that the action to which the person is being incited seems in the moment to be very attractive and the urge to do it almost overwhelming. But if someone acts on a *shaytanic* impulse it very soon becomes apparent that it was a great mistake and usually leads to a feeling of burning regret but also leaves them less able to resist the next time. The apparent strength of the *shaytanic* impulse is, however, simply that, nothing but an appearance and if someone is on the lookout for it and recognises it when it appears, it is easily repulsed. All someone has to do if they are attacked by an impulse from *Shaytan* is to sincerely seek refuge with Allah from it and they will find that it disappears as if in a puff of smoke. We find in the Qur'an:

> *If an evil impulse from Shaytan provokes you,*
> *seek refuge in Allah.*
> *He is All-Hearing, All-Seeing.*
> *As for those who are godfearing,*
> *when they are bothered by visitors from Shaytan,*
> *they remember and immediately see clearly.*
> *But as for their brothers,*
> *they lead them further into error.*
> *And they do not stop at that!* (7:200-202)

SHAHAWAT – APPETITES

The third of the five factors which can prevent the human heart from becoming aware of the Divine Presence is the physical appetites – in Arabic, *shahawat*. These comprise the natural animal appetites needed for the preservation of human life and include such things as the desire for food and drink, sex and sleep, and basic instincts like that of aggressive energy. All of these are clearly necessary and so there is no question of eliminating them altogether. It is only when they are indulged excessively and start to dominate the being that they become harmful. Provided they are kept in balance and allowed to fulfil their natural functions they are nothing but beneficial and the key to ensuring that this occurs and that they do not become a hindrance lies in keeping them within the clear limits laid down by Islamic law.

The desire for food is obviously essential for the continued life of every human being and it is only when it is consumed to excess or people become obsessed with it that it becomes detrimental. The basic legal requirement for food is that it must be *halal* and *tayyib* – permitted and wholesome – and since very few foods are prohibited there is little restriction from the purely legal standpoint. There are, however, warnings against over-consumption in the Qur'an and in several hadiths. We find, for instance, in *Surat al-A'raf*:

> ... and eat and drink but do not go to excess.
> He (Allah) does not love the profligate. (7:29)

And there is a hadith in Sahih al-Bukhari in which it is related from Abu Hurayra that a man used to eat a lot. He became Muslim and then he used to eat a little. That was mentioned to the Prophet 🕮 and he said, "The believer eats in one intestine and the unbeliever eats in seven." In the *Jami'* of at-Tirmidhi there is another hadith in which Abu Karima al-Miqdam ibn Ma'dikarib said, "I heard the Messenger of Allah 🕮 say, 'A human being fills up no vessel worse than his belly. Enough for a son of Adam are some morsels which will keep his back straight. If it cannot be avoided, then a third is for his food, a third for his drink, and a third for his breath (i.e. should be left empty).'" What is clear from this is that food is one of the great blessings of Allah and that it should be enjoyed, but only in moderation.

Desire for more food than you need to satisfy your hunger is called greed and this can spill over into other areas of life. If it turns into a desire for someone else's property and that desire is acted upon it becomes theft. It can also take the form of commercial greed in which case it is usually expressed in terms of usurious transactions and monopolisation. Each of these is dealt with specifically and fiercely under Islamic law. Another way that greed is legislated against in Islam is through the detailed laws of inheritance specified in the Qur'an which ensure that inherited wealth is equitably distributed among a person's heirs and prevents the excessive build-up of wealth in the hands of a few. This provision alone has enormous significance to us living as we do in an era witnessing the ravages of an unbounded capitalism based on the acquisition and retention of wealth by increasingly fewer people at the expense of the impoverishment of the vast majority of the earth's peoples.

Where drinking is concerned all intoxicating substances are forbidden. Concern about the growing consumption of alcohol is now being expressed in the media on an almost daily basis. It is clear that in the case of alcohol, limiting consumption by recommending moderation is not an option. Allah says in an *ayat* of the Qur'an that although there is some benefit in alcohol the harm definitely outweighs the benefit and experience has shown that human beings are not able to restrict themselves to its beneficial aspects and it is having an ever more devastating effect in societies throughout the world.

Scenes played out weekly in almost every city centre throughout the Western world show how it reduces thousands of young people to bestial or even sub-animal behaviour, while at the same time middle-aged, middle-class people in their homes consume increasing amounts of wine and spirits unaware of the destruction they wreak on their health and lives. It is recognised that a vast proportion of the crime, both violent and otherwise, and including domestic crime such as wife-beating and worse, which has reached such epidemic proportions in our time, is closely related to the consumption of alcohol and drugs. If you add to this the vast percentage of alcohol-induced accidents, the growing incidence of alcoholism with its attendant social problems and the unprecedented number of people dependant on drugs of all kinds, the Qu'ranic injunction forbidding intoxicants and the penalty for publicly contravening it needs no further elucidation. We have dwelt at some length on alcohol, although we acknowledge the similar dangers inherent in all intoxicants, simply because the scale of the harm inflicted by alcohol vastly outweighs that due to other drugs and intoxicants that are more sensational in the eyes of the media.

The human sexual appetite is still obviously necessary for the successful continuation of the human species – despite anything modern scientific advances in the fields of IVF and cloning technology might want us to believe to the contrary. It is, however, equally obvious that, from the mythical mists of early human history down to the present day, the human sexual drive has also had the potential to be an immensely powerful destructive force both for society and the individual, as untold evidence from the Fall of Troy through to the alarming current statistics on the unprecedented occurrence of rape, paedophilia, incest and marriage breakdown in the world today makes abundantly clear. Nor can it be denied that the spread of the pandemic of AIDS which now threatens so many millions of lives has been almost exclusively due to sexual promiscuity on a scale never before witnessed by the human race.

Again, in this vital area of life the legal limits of Islam hold the key. Far from being suppressed, the sexual appetite is explicitly encouraged within Islam and ample space is given for its expression. However its limits have been made clear and the penalties for overstepping them extremely severe. At the same time, opportunities for sex outside the prescribed limits are kept to a minimum.

An important point to make here, especially in the light of the current debate about Muslim dress at schools and elsewhere, is that the Islamic rulings regarding dress both for men and women must be seen in the context of protection for the individual and society from the kind of sexual excesses so prevalent in modern society. The wearing of a headscarf by Muslim girls must be seen in this context; it is not a matter of cultural identity. It should also be seen in the context of a traditional Muslim society in which both men and women would dress modestly, and both cover their heads. Another thing which should be stated here is that, although homosexual behaviour is recognised as a human possibility, its practice is categorically prohibited under Islamic law.

The appetite for sleep is probably the least prone of the natural appetites to excessive indulgence although there is no doubt that if it is overindulged it has a detrimental effect on both individuals and society. Excessive sleep is automatically precluded by the simple antidote of doing the five daily prayers of Islam at the prescribed time. Provided the prayers are done on time, it is almost impossible to envisage a scenario in which sleep could become harmful on an individual or social level.

A certain amount of aggressive energy on the part of human beings is necessary to get things done but it becomes destructive when, as all too frequently happens, it turns to anger and violence. The Qur'anic legislation regarding retaliation and blood money is specifically intended to counteract the harmful effects of excessive human anger and there are several hadiths which directly address the problem. For instance the Prophet ﷺ said, "If one of you gets angry and he is standing he should sit down until his anger subsides and if it does not he should lie down." (Ahmad, Abu Dawud, al-Bayhaqi)

The main point to take from all this is that the thrust of the greater part of Islamic law is the protection of both Muslim society and the individual Muslim from the harmful effects which inevitably ensue when natural human characteristics are taken to excess, when natural behavioural limits are overstepped. It is interesting in this regard that many of the penalties for the crimes which stem from this are known as *hudud* whose normal meaning in Arabic is "frontier". So they represent, as it were, those points at which human behaviour goes beyond the point of acceptable human norms. Provided

The Natural Form of Man

people remain within the borders of the behavioural territory mapped out by the injunctions of Islamic law and avoid transgressing beyond the frontiers marked out so distinctly by the Divinely ordained penalties they safeguard themselves both on a social and individual basis. It is a part of the wisdom of Islam that one not even approach these limits, for fear of transgressing them. Reflecting this we find a Qur'anic injunction in *Surat al-Baqara* when we are told:

These are Allah's limits, so do not go near them. (2:186)

And there is one hadith from the Prophet 🕌 which truly makes this whole matter wonderfully clear:

An-Nu'man ibn Bashir said, "I heard the Messenger of Allah 🕌 say, 'What is permitted is clear and what is prohibited is clear. But between the two there are doubtful things about which most people have no knowledge. Whoever exercises caution with regard to what is doubtful, shows prudence in respect of his *deen* and his honour. Whoever gets involved in the doubtful things is like a herdsman who grazes his animals near a private preserve (*hima*). He is bound to enter it. Every king has a private preserve and the private preserve of Allah on His earth are the things that He has made forbidden. There is a lump of flesh in the body, the nature of which is that when it is sound, the entire body is sound, and when it is corrupt, the entire body is corrupt – it is the heart.'" (Al-Bukhari and Muslim)

From this we know that the core aim of all the legislative injunctions of Islam is the protection and purification of the human heart.

HAWA – SUBTLE DESIRES OF THE SELF

The fourth of the five factors which obstruct the heart is *hawa* – subtle desires which manifest themselves as blameworthy characteristics such as pride, ingratitude, conceit, envy, showing-off, anxiety and similar negative character traits. The difference between these and the appetites we have been looking at is that these characteristics are acquired whereas the appetites are innate. Children are born in need of food and drink and sleep but no child is born arrogant or envious or conceited. Such characteristics are developed during the course of people's life in this world. Because of this it is in fact far easier to protect the heart from the harmful effects of the physical appetites than from these character defects which are more intertwined with a person's individual identity and consequently more difficult to eradicate. It is worth taking a brief look at some of these traits to understand their nature and how the heart can be purified from them.

PRIDE

'Abdullah ibn Mas'ud reported that the Prophet 🕌 said, "No one who has an atom's weight of pride in his heart will enter the Garden." A man said, "And if a man likes his clothes to be good and his sandals to be good?" He said, "Allah is Beautiful and loves beauty. Pride means to renounce the truth and abase people." (Muslim) This hadith tells us all we need to know about the blameworthy nature of pride. The essence of pride is to consider yourself superior to someone else and this is in fact the real original sin since it is the cause of *Shaytan* being banished from the presence of Allah. When he was commanded to prostrate before Adam, *Shaytan* replied: "*I am better than him. You created me from fire and You created him from clay.*" (7:12) Allah then said to him: "*Descend from Heaven. It is not for you to be arrogant in it. So get out! You are one of the abased.*" (7:13)

The reason that pride is so destructive to the heart is that it precludes the possibility of a person having humility which is the necessary condition for all virtue. It means that a person is arrogating to themselves a quality that in reality is the sole province of their Creator and by doing that cut themselves off from any possibility of true worship of their Lord. Abu Hurayra reported that the Messenger of Allah ﷺ said, "Allah, the Mighty and Exalted, said, 'Might is My wrapper, and pride is My cloak and I will punish anyone who contends with me [for them].'" (Muslim)

INGRATITUDE

"If you are ungrateful Allah is rich beyond need of any of you and He is not pleased with ingratitude in His slaves. But if you are grateful He is pleased with you for that." (39:8) Ingratitude is another of the bad qualities whose presence prevent people's hearts from awareness of their Lord. It manifests as discontentment with one's lot in life and complaint about one's circumstances. This demonstrates deep ignorance of the nature of existence because it means that you think things should be other than the way that Allah has decreed they will be and also implies that you think that you could do a better job than the Creator of the universe.

The truth is that everything we have is a gift from Allah, our existence itself and all our sustenance, but we tend to attribute the things we like to ourselves and anything we dislike becomes a source of complaint. *"If We let man taste mercy from Us, and then take it away from him, he is despairing, ungrateful; but if We let him taste blessings after hardship has afflicted him, he says, 'My troubles have gone away,' and he is overjoyed, boastful."* (11:9-10)

It is worthy of note that the Arabic word for ingratitude is *kufr* which is the same word that is often translated as disbelief. This key Arabic term means in its root to "cover over", and in the context of disbelief "to cover over the blessings of Allah" i.e. to be ungrateful. In extremes it means also to reject. This rejection of the Divine has as its beginning point simple ingratitude.

CONCEIT

Conceit is sometimes confused with pride but the two are quite different. The proud person always needs another to be superior to whereas with a conceited person it is a matter of themselves alone. They are the kind of people who think they can do no wrong but that is the greatest self-delusion. "*Say: 'Shall I inform you of the greatest losers respecting their actions? People whose efforts in the life of this world are misguided while they suppose that they are doing good.'*" (18:99) Conceit is such a destructive force in the heart because the conceited person is above all concerned with affirming their own identity and, by doing that, making their own selves a barrier between themselves and their Lord. They literally idolise themselves, turn themselves into the object of their own worship. We find in the Qur'an: "*Have you seen him who has taken his whims and desires to be his god?*" (25:43)

ENVY

Envy is one of the most destructive qualities it is possible for a human heart to house. We are instructed in the Qur'an to seek Allah's protection from it: "*...and from the evil of an envier when he envies.*" (113:5) The Prophet 🕊 said of it: "Beware of envy. Envy devours good actions as fire devours wood" (or he said, "dry grass"). (Abu Dawud)

There are different degrees of envy. There is the envy when someone resents what someone else has and both desires it for themselves and to deprive the other person of it. This is the worst kind of envy. There is the envy of wanting what someone else has without wanting to deprive them of it. There is also the kind of envy displayed by someone who resents what someone else has but realises that they cannot have it and so they want the other person to lose it so that they can be the same. All these are destructive to the heart.

The Prophet 🕊 gave permission for envy in two instances: Ibn Mas'ud reported that the Prophet 🕊 said, "You can only have envy in two situations: you may envy a man to whom Allah has given wealth which he spends for the sake of the truth, and a man to whom Allah has given wisdom which he both acts by and teaches." (Al-Bukhari and Muslim)

SHOWING-OFF

Another widespread and adverse negative quality is that of showing-off. Showing-off means acting in order to be noticed by others. This is something that is often deeply embedded in the human psyche and originates in the very earliest days of the emergence of the individuated self-form. One of the ways in which people begin to realise their own individual identity is through the way they are affirmed, or indeed negated, by those around them and they start to act in ways which will elicit a particular reaction to reinforce the idea of themselves which they are in the process of building up. This basic patterning tends to be perpetuated as people grow up and gradually forms an integral part of their personality and of the way they relate to the world.

In practical terms this means that most of the actions which many people do are done with the object of gaining either the approval or disapproval of people around them. Unfortunately this tendency is frequently so deeply rooted that it also extends to acts of worship and other actions whose ostensible object is Allah alone and this is why it is so destructive to the heart. We know that actions are dependent on the intention behind them and if they are done for something other than Allah they are not acceptable as acts of worship. If there is any element of showing-off connected with the action concerned it will be by definition defective with respect to its intention and therefore of no benefit to the worshipper. *"Anyone who associates something with Allah has gone very far astray."* (4:116)

ANXIETY

Anxiety is another thing which frequently troubles the heart. We find in the Qur'an:

> *Whereas another group became prey to anxious thoughts,*
> *thinking other than the truth about Allah*
> *thoughts belonging to the Days of Ignorance –*
> *saying, "Do we have any say in the affair at all?"*
> *Say, "The affair belongs entirely to Allah."* (3:154)

This clearly shows us the nature of anxiety, revealing it to be, like ingratitude, a matter of ignorance. The difference between the two is that ingratitude is ignorance combined with anger whereas anxiety is ignorance combined with fear. The fear is of things somehow going wrong or of not getting what you need. This is ignorance because the truth is that "*The affair belongs entirely to Allah*" and believers know that it is not in the nature of their Lord to let them down: "*Allah would not let your belief go to waste. Allah is All-Gentle, Most Merciful to mankind.*" (2:142)

Anxiety comes from not really believing that Allah is in control of existence, from lack of trust in Allah, from lack of true knowledge of the Divine Unity. It frequently manifests itself as anxiety about provision, as fear that we will not get what we need to feed, clothe and house ourselves adequately, so that anxiety about employment or lack of it, about income or shortage of it, is what in fact occupies most people's hearts and minds and cuts them off from the possibility of active awareness of the presence of Allah.

This has been a brief and somewhat cursory look at just a few, among many others, of those negative characteristics which can sully the human heart and which need to be eliminated if the individual concerned is to have a hope of gaining the purity of heart necessary for the formulation of the truly sincere intention essential for acceptable acts of worship. They are referred to generally in the Qur'an as sicknesses of the heart and so purification from them is a kind of healing process. For healing to take place two things are needed: the right medicine and a skilful doctor to prescribe and administer it.

THE NEED FOR A TEACHER

Every branch of knowledge requires teachers who are thoroughly versed in it to pass it on to those who wish to learn it and the knowledge of *ihsan* is no different from any other in this respect. In fact for this science a teacher is more vital than for almost any other, most of which can be picked up to some extent from books even if there are inevitably perils associated with that. In the case of *ihsan* it is absolutely necessary to have teachers who have gone through the whole purification process themselves so that they will be able to recognise the problems faced by the students under them and be able to show them how to overcome them based on their own experience.

The process of the purification of the heart is often seen as a journey through unknown territory and the teacher as the guide on that journey. A guide is only of any use if he has already made the journey before and knows the way and so is able to tell you what you need to take with you and point out the dangers and bring you safely to your destination.

The point is that many of the characteristics which obstruct a person's heart are so inextricably bound up with their identity that, in the first place, it is often very difficult for them to recognise them at all and, even when they do, getting free of them by sheer dint of one's own knowledge and exertions can be a complex and arduous task. A teacher who has already been through the process will be able to recognise the exact nature of the particular sickness involved and will be able to prescribe the exact cure needed in the specific case in front of him.

The teaching of *ihsan* has been going on continuously since the time of the Prophet ﷺ and has been firmly based in the Book and *Sunna* during all that time. Its two pillars have always been *dhikrullah* – remembrance/invocation of Allah – and keeping company.

DHIKR – REMEMBRANCE OF ALLAH

There are many references in the Qur'an to *dhikr*. Two representative *ayats* are.

> *O you who believe, remember Allah much.*
> *And glorify Him in the morning and the evening.* (33:41-2)

Say: "Allah misguides anyone He wills
and guides to Himself all who turn to Him:
those who believe and whose hearts
are stilled by the remembrance of Allah.
Only by the remembrance of Allah
can the hearts be stilled." (13:28-9)

So the general remedy of *dhikrullah* is essential for all who wish to purify their hearts and has been prescribed by all who have taught this knowledge since the time of the Prophet ﷺ. Another universally recommended practice mentioned several times in the Qur'an is getting up during the last part of the night before dawn to pray and invoke Allah and ask for blessings on the Messenger of Allah ﷺ and make supplication to Allah. Each teacher, however, has a particular form of invocation, known as a *wird*, which will differ from one teacher to another, and which they give to all their students. It is normally done by each student on a twice daily basis and acts as a constantly renewed connection with the teacher they follow. They also hold gatherings, often on a weekly basis, at which groups of their students meet to remember Allah together. In addition to this most teachers will prescribe specific practices for individual students according to their particular requirements. They are able to see the ways in which each student is being impeded on their path of self purification and will give them clear guidance as to how they can free their hearts from those bad qualities which are holding up their progress.

HUBB AD-DUNYA – LOVE OF THE WORLD

This brings us to the last of the heart's obstructions: love of this world. Just as the experiencing self (*nafs*) is the seat of the other elements – *Shaytan*, the appetites and negative qualities of character – which prevent the heart from becoming aware of the Divine Presence, love of this world is what results from them. The Arabic word for heart, *qalb*, derives from the verb *qalaba*, which means to turn around, and this gives an indication of the true nature of the heart. Allah says in the Qur'an: "*Allah has not allotted to any man two hearts within his breast.*" (33:4) The human heart can only face in one direction at any one time. Either, in its impure state, it is facing towards this world, unable to escape from it, or, when purified, it turns towards Allah, no longer imprisoned by this world, free to worship Allah with absolute sincerity.

The thirteenth-century Egyptian scholar and poet Muhammad al-Busayri made an illuminating simile for this process in his great poem *al-Burda*: "The *nafs* is like an infant, if you leave it alone, it will never come off the breast but if you wean it, it will be weaned." The breast here represents this world and weaning refers to the purification of the heart. We talked earlier of how the human self is not as fixed as we often think and is in reality quite fluid and open to radical transformation. Reflecting this and based on reference to it in the Qur'an, the *nafs* is described in various ways according to the stage of purification it has reached. There is no reason why a particular individual should not progress through some, or in certain rare cases all, of the defined stages.

An-nafs al-ammara — the commanding self

In its most opaque state, that of unbelieving people totally cut off from Allah, the human self is given the name *an-nafs al-ammara* – the commanding self – taken from the Qur'anic *ayat*: "*The lower self commands to evil acts – except for those my Lord has mercy on.*" (12:53) In this state the self has little or no self reflective capacity and so is unaware of its own state of sickness. It is, therefore, helplessly subject to its own worst impulses and unable even to see that it is acting wrongly and self destructively. Any self restraint displayed is purely for reasons of social convention or fear of legal retribution, not for any real understanding of wrongdoing.

An-nafs al-lawwama — the self-reproaching self

In the next stage it is called *an-nafs al-lawwama* – the self-reproaching self – taken from the Qur'anic *ayat*: "*No! I swear by the self-reproaching self.*" (75:2) It should be noted here that the scholars of Qur'anic commentary have said that the simple fact of Allah swearing an oath by this stage of the self means that it is a tremendous matter, since Allah only swears oaths by creations of His that are great. At this stage the person concerned is at least vaguely aware of their own faults and has some inner consciousness of the difference between right and wrong action. They may still be firmly attached to this world but accept that they will be answerable in the Next World for their actions here. They lack self control and veer between acts of base self gratification and acts of obedience to Allah without any real ability to keep themselves on a straight course.

AN-NAFS AL-MULHAMA – THE INSPIRED SELF

The name given to the self in the third stage is *an-nafs al-mulhama* – the inspired self – taken from the Qur'anic *ayats*: "*And the self and what proportioned it and inspired it with depravity or godliness. He who purifies it has succeeded. He who covers it up has failed.*" (91:7-10) At this stage the person involved has reached a point when their heart is sufficiently purified to be able to clearly discriminate between what will bring them benefit and what will cause them harm and, moreover, to choose those actions which are beneficial rather than harmful for them. Such people's hearts are on a pivot, swinging between this world and the light of their Lord. This is the state of people firmly established on the path of purification.

AN-NAFS AL-MUTMA'INNA – THE SERENE SELF

At the fourth stage the self is called *an-nafs al-mutma'inna* – the serene self – taken from the Qur'anic *ayat*: "*O self at rest and at peace (mutma'inna) return to your Lord well-pleasing and well-pleased!*" (89:30-1) These are people who have completely purified their hearts. Love of this world has left their hearts and although they continue to participate fully in life their hearts are turned permanently towards their Lord. Nothing is now able to disturb their luminous serenity. They have become still points in time and space, a locus of lights, where the timeless, spaceless light of Allah is reflected and remembered continually.

AN-NAFS AL-KAMILA — THE PERFECTED SELF

There is one further stage reached only by the most elect of the elite in which the human self becomes *an-nafs al-kamila* – the perfected self. This is the state of the Messenger of Allah ﷺ and in a subordinate way that of those who have followed him with authorisation from Allah and his Messenger ﷺ to pass on the core of the Message he brought. They are not just windows looking out onto the light of Allah; they are doorways giving others direct access to that light, illuminated and illuminating, guided by Allah and guiding to Allah, reminding other people of Him and of the path laid down by the Messenger of Allah which leads to Him. Shaykh Ibn 'Ata'illah al-Iskandari says of them in his seminal text *al-Hikam*: "Glory be to Him who makes His 'friends' known only because it is a way of making Himself known and only takes a person to them when He wants to bring them to Himself."

Up to this point we have been looking at the knowledge of *ihsan* from a microcosmic viewpoint, at how it affects the individual Muslim. It is also necessary, however, to take a macrocosmic view of it and to look at it in a more universal way. The contemporary teacher Shaykh Abdalqadir as-Sufi, says as part of his definition of sufism, and therefore *ihsan*, at the beginning of his book *The Hundred Steps*:

Sufism is the science of the journey to the King... It is taking the ancient way, the primordial path of direct experience of the Real.

The sufi is universal. He has reduced and then eliminated the marks of selfhood to allow a clear view of the cosmic reality. He has rolled up the cosmos in its turn and obliterated it. He has gone beyond. The sufi has said "Allah" – until he has understood.

The meaning of these words will be further amplified during the course of this discussion. Shaykh Muhammad ibn al-Habib, the teacher of Shaykh Abdalqadir, says with reference to *ihsan* in a long supplication he wrote:

We ask for an *ihsan* which will drive us into the presence of the unseen worlds and which will purify us from every kind of heedlessness and defect.

The Shaykh speaks here about the presence of unseen worlds and he also speaks about forgetfulness and defects. This brings us immediately face to face with two very different paths human beings can follow in their lives. The word for human being in Arabic is *insan*. One meaning of this word is the pupil of the eye; another etymological possibility is that it comes from the word which means to forget. So the word itself contains the two directions which a human being can take. One possibility is that we become completely engrossed in this world, forgetting that our life in it is merely part of a much longer journey which started before we were born and will continue beyond our death. The other possibility open to us is that, like the pupil of the eye, we become a lens, except that whereas the pupil stands as the interface between the outer world of forms and the inner world of sense perception, the human being as a whole stands potentially as the conscious interface between this material world and the unseen world of spiritual realities.

So how does it come about that the human being holds this exalted position in the scheme of things? There are three sayings the first of which is authentically attributed to the Prophet Muhammad 🌸 which together make up a complete description of the true nature of existence and of our place as human beings in it and which take us to the very root of our humanness and put us beyond all the evolutionary or historical definitions to which we have become so accustomed.

The first is the hadith narrated by Imam al-Bukhari: "Allah was and there was nothing with Him" to which, when it was narrated in his presence, Imam al-Junayd added the logical corollary, "and He is as He was."

The second is words attributed to Allah: "I was a hidden treasure and I desired to be known. So I created the creation in order to be known."[1]

And the third is: "My heaven does not contain Me nor My earth but the heart of My believing slave contains Me."[2]

"Allah was and there was nothing with Him." The current climate of opinion has turned the existence of God into a matter of philosophical speculation with the result that for most people, including many who consider themselves believers, the existence of God has been turned into a speculative hypothesis. How far this is from the Truth! The existence of Allah is the most absolute certainty. Not, it is true, the distant, capricious, potentate God of misinterpreted scripture but Reality itself, that Oneness on Whom everything is totally and continually dependant for its being, but Who is Himself beyond need of anything – Oneness, not in the arithmetical

---

1 Mulla 'Ali al-Qari said that the meaning of the statement, "I was a hidden treasure and I desired to be known. So I created the creation in order to be known," is authentic and corresponds to the *ayat* of Qur'an in which Allah, exalted is He, said, "*I only created jinn and man to worship Me.*" (51:52) Worship in this *ayat* was interpreted by the Companion Ibn 'Abbas ﷺ to mean "to have knowledge (*ma'rifa*) of" in the sense of the gnostic recognition of Allah.

2 "My heaven does not contain Me nor My earth but the heart of My believing slave contains Me," although widely quoted as a hadith of the Prophet ﷺ is narrated as a saying of Ezekiel by Ahmad ibn Hanbal in *Kitab az-zuhd* from Wahb ibn Munabbih as, "The heavens and the earth are too weak to encompass Me, and the heart of My soft calm believing slave encompasses Me." The sense of this is also confirmed by a hadith of the Messenger of Allah ﷺ transmitted by ad-Daraqutni.

sense of being the first of two or three but rather that absolute singularity which does not permit the independent existence of anything else alongside it. Everything else comes into existence and goes out of it again, begins and ends, is born and dies. Allah is before and after. There is no beginning to His firstness, no end to His lastness. Nothing is like Him or can be compared with Him nor is it possible to have any conception of what He is like.

"And He is as He was." If this is the case how do we exist at all and are now living on this planet which is part of the solar system in one of countless galaxies in a universe which seems to go on for ever? The answer to this question is that the absolute, majestic and overwhelming transcendence of the first tradition is conditioned by the second: "I was a hidden treasure and I desired to be known. So I created the creation in order to be known." It was the desire to be known expressed in the depths of the Essence of the Divine Being that caused the process of creation and led to the unfolding of the many layers of existence and all the forms contained in them including ourselves and the universe we inhabit.

Another tradition about the actual moment of creation says that when Allah decreed that the creation should come into existence out of non-existence, He grasped a handful of His light and said to it, "Be Muhammad!" And then from that light He created everything else in existence.

Now we have to be careful when we hear this that we do not dismiss it by considering it to be merely a figure of speech or a poetic metaphor. It is literally what happened. Shaykh Muhammad ibn al-Habib says in his *Diwan* at the beginning of the *qasida* entitled the *Qualities of Muhammad*:

> Muhammad is the fountain-head of lights and darkness
>   and the source of their emergence
>   from the presence of before-time.
> So his light was the first of lights when He determined
>   the manifestation of His Names in the first world.

> From him all things were clothed
>   in their origination in being,
>   and their support comes from him
>   without any interruption.

And this, of course, as it applies to the whole of existence, also applies to our own universe and everything in it including our own emergence as human beings on the earth. Again be careful you do not take this as metaphor; it is a literal description of how things have come into existence.

Taking the present state of the expanding universe and working backwards from it, cosmologists, both astronomers and quantum physicists, have come up with a more or less consistent picture of the first moments of the universe. They say that the universe developed from a singularity, an infinitely small, infinitely dense point emerging out of nothingness. It was a fireball, they say, and by that they mean, of course, not fire as we know it today, but rather a ball of pure energy. Its rate of expansion was incredibly fast as we understand time now but because in those early moments space and time were inextricably bound up together we can have no real idea of what the conditions were like within it. The important point for us in the present context is that the whole event in these very early stages is described by the cosmologists as being made up of undifferentiated light.

So what has, through the aeons of expansion, turned into innumerable galaxies made up of stars and planets, a few of which are visible to us when we look up into the breathtaking beauty of the sky at night, was all potentially present, in a latent form, in this ball of light. Because of the inconceivable degree of chance necessary to bring about the conditions which made our emergence as sentient human beings on this planet a possibility, the scientists have developed a theory they call the anthropic principle. They say that if we take as a starting point the fact that human beings exist, all the principle qualities of the universe, all the natural laws, even all the physical constants, can be derived from this fact. If the universe had developed in an even infinitesimally different way human existence would not have been possible. In other words what they are saying is that the only possible conclusion is that the whole universe was brought about so that human beings could come into existence, so that they, in turn, would be able to describe the universe.

In the thirteenth century, the Andalusian Shaykh Muhyi'd-din ibn 'Arabi, whose family came from Murcia in Spain and who himself lived for the first part of his life in Seville, enunciated clearly what was in any case common knowledge among the Muslims: "In the universe it was man who was intended." This was, of course, because they knew that the first impulse of creation took the form of the Muhammadan Light: in other words they understood that the whole purpose of existence was the coming into being of the perfect human form which became physically manifest in the succession of incorruptible Messengers and Prophets of Allah who reached their apogee and fulfilment with the advent of the Prophet Muhammad ﷺ. That was the mirror in which the "Hidden Treasure" became known by revealing Himself to Himself in all His Majesty and Beauty.

Now we are approaching the core of the matter of *ihsan*: what Shaykh Abdalqadir referred to as "the journey to the King". Knowledge of our universe forms part of it, but only a very small part. Shaykh Muhammad ibn al-Habib says in his *Great Ode* about the person making this journey:

> He would see the planets
>   and the secrets of their constellations
> and the meaning
>   of their tremendously rapid movement.

But even this becomes insignificant when compared with the scale of the journey as a whole because he continues:

> The veil of the tablet of forms
>   would be lifted from his secret
> and so the hidden sciences would emerge uncovered.

– Had the trees been the pens to write it
  and their ink all of the surrounding seas,
they would have dried up –
And he would visit the domain which is peopled by
  the limitless array of innumerable angels,

And further:

He would freely roam around
  the Throne and the Footstool
which make the heavenly bodies
  appear like a small ring.

With reference to this last statement the great early Muslim gnostic, Abu Yazid al-Bistami, said when describing his own path to knowledge that as he rose through the seven heavens, the size of each of them in comparison with the succeeding one was like that of a ring thrown into a desert. Then he reached the Throne of Allah, which is the greatest of all created forms and he said of it that it disappeared into a corner of his heart. This shows us what an extraordinary thing a human being is; what human possibilities really are. And the most astonishing thing is that what the Shaykh Muhammad ibn al-Habib has referred to is just the preliminary stage of the journey. He then goes on to say:

And, in his quest to purify
  the secret of his secret from every delay,
  he finally stops at the door to the pure Presence.
This station of the People
  in the journey of their spirits
  is the station of concealment and bewilderment.
After it comes knowledge –
  which may not be disseminated
except by the one who in vision
  has received a clear authority.

So the gnostic knowledge we are talking about only begins

after this vast inner-outer journey has been brought to its completion. Finally the Shaykh says, echoing the final tradition about the heart of the believer:

> So there are signs in the self for any who ponders it
>   because all existence is contained in it.
> In purification the self expands to contain the Real.
>   Now do not wonder and ask
> 'How?' or 'Where?' or 'What?'

Now the words of Shaykh Abdalqadir as-Sufi quoted earlier:

> He has reduced and then eliminated the marks of selfhood to allow a clear view of the cosmic reality. He has rolled up the cosmos in its turn and obliterated it. He has gone beyond.

Now these words can be seen in their true perspective. Men who achieve this exalted station have clear authority to impart what they know and are indeed obliged to convey their knowledge in order to guide other human beings to the path of Allah.

He says in *The Hundred Steps* about this ultimate human possibility, about direct knowledge of Allah itself:

MA'RIFA – GNOSIS

Gnosis is the knowledge on which all other knowledge rests. All knowledges are suppositional yet verifiable in the realm of contingency. This knowledge is real yet not demonstrable. Other knowledges do not, however, illuminate their knower, nor remove his anguish, nor give him judgement in every case, nor invest his presence with light and radiance. The man of knowledge remains in needs and creational dependence. The man of gnosis does not remain in any need except dependency on his Lord Who gives him what he requires from creation. Other knowledges, being constructs without foundation, are baseless. Gnosis, the central knowledge, for it is knowledge of the self, is a proof to the one who knows it and this is its glory and its supremacy over all others. By it, its possessor knows the Universe, how it is set up and its underlying laws in their action, their qualities and their essences. His knowledge of the Universe is his own self knowledge, while his knowledge of his own self is direct perception of his own original reality, his Adamic identity. Everything he has comes from Allah. He never sees anything but he sees Allah in it, before it, after it. There is only Allah in his eyes as in his heart.

Whoever has gained this has gained the red sulphur. By it he can transform the hearts of those who come to him, for his presence alone is a guidance and a reminder. He guides to Allah by Allah.

And as Shaykh Abdalqadir makes clear in his book, this ultimate knowledge is in fact the beginning of another phase of endless unveilings in which, as he says, the secrets of love flow without end. And, looking at it from a slightly different angle, Shaykh Muhammad ibn al-Habib says about it in the *qasida* we have been looking at:

A man would not hesitate to spend all he had
 – if he only recognised the secret of his own heart.
If a man could but grasp the bliss of his secret
 he would shed a tear with every breath he breathed.

This has hopefully been enough to give us at least an idea of what *ihsan*, the true birthright of the realised human being, entails. But, of course, for those in whose beings a chord has been struck, for those who feel a stirring in their hearts towards this highest human possibility, an idea is not enough; they will only be satisfied by the experience itself. But such ultimate fulfilment does not come cheap. The price is very high. Shaykh Abdalqadir alludes to it when he says, talking of the man who achieves the goal: "He has reduced and then eliminated the marks of selfhood…" This is referring to the path of purification of the self we examined earlier which forms the necessary preliminary stages of the journey to the King. But for this too there is a necessary precondition and that is the basic act of submission which every human being must make and this brings us back to the hadith of the Prophet ﷺ about Islam, Iman and Ihsan with which we started.

Shaykh Abdalqadir says at the very beginning of *The Hundred Steps*:

> 'There is no road to the realities except on the tongue of the *shari'a*,' said Shaykh al-Akbar. The *shari'a* of Islam is the confirmation that there is no divinity but Allah and that Muhammad ﷺ is the Messenger of Allah. It is to pray five times daily the ritual prostrations. It is to fast the month of Ramadan. It is to pay the *zakat* tax of wealth. It is to take, if possible, the *Hajj* to the pure House of Allah and the plain of 'Arafat. It is based on these and confirms that the one following the *shari'a* has elected to live within the broad moral parameters set down in the Qur'anic commands and according to the guidance within the *Sunna*, the life pattern of Muhammad ﷺ.

So adopting the divinely ordained framework of Islam, becoming a Muslim, is the necessary first step for someone who wants to set out on this path of self-knowledge; it is the gateway which must be gone through to make the journey we have been talking about possible. But as the Shaykh makes clear, this does not involve saddling oneself with some arbitrarily imposed set of laws but is in itself just a further recognition of what it is to be a human being. He says that by becoming a Muslim and accepting Allah's limits as conveyed to us by His final Messenger Muhammad ﷺ we are simply recognising:

> ...that the human creature is limited, is in a body, and thus like all bodies in the physical world is subject to given laws. ... (so the legal framework of Islam) is the self-chosen pattern of life one has adopted in order to deepen knowledge until one reaches one's own source,

one's spring of life, to drink the water of illumination. It implies the recognition of biological laws that function at every level of existence.

The choice facing each human being is, therefore, very straight-forward: either to go one's own way, following one's own whims and desires, and by doing that to deny oneself the possibility of any permanent satisfaction or peace of mind and condemn oneself to an eternity of burning regret for having missed the chance; or to go in through this door and follow the path of Allah and His Messengers which leads, in any case, to the pleasure of Allah and also opens the way to the glorious possibility of that gnostic knowledge we have been talking about, which is both the ultimate purpose and the complete fulfilment of human existence. We have to go one way or the other. There is no third way. The choice is ours.

Glossary of Arabic Terms and Names

ahkam:	judgements, rulings.
Ansar:	the "Helpers", the people of Madina who welcomed and aided the Prophet.
'Asr:	the Afternoon Prayer.
ayat:	a verse of the Qur'an.
Azra'il:	the angel of death
barazkh:	the interspatial life in the grave between death in this world and resurrection on the Day of Rising.
deen:	the life-transaction, lit. the debt between two parties; in this usage between the Creator and created.
dhikr:	remembrance, invocation of Allah.
Dhuhr:	the Midday Prayer.
Eid:	a festival, either the festival at the end of Ramadan or at the time of the Hajj.
Fatiha:	"the Opener", the first *sura* of the Qur'an.
fiqh:	knowledge of what actions are obligatory, forbidden, recommended, disapproved or permissible.
fuqaha:	people knowledgeable in *fiqh*.
ghusl:	major ablution of the whole body with water required to regain purity after menstruation,

lochia and sexual intercourse.

hadith: an account narrated of something that the Prophet ﷺ did, said or was present at. The hadith cited in this book are followed by mention in parentheses of the source in which they are found, e.g. (Muslim) indicates that the hadith came from the collection of Imam Muslim.

Hajj: the annual pilgrimage to Makka which is one of the five pillars of Islam.

Hajji: someone who has performed the *hajj*.

halal: permitted by the *Shari'a*.

haram: forbidden by the *Shari'a*.

Haram: Sacred Precinct, a protected area in which certain behaviour is forbidden and other behaviour necessary. The area around the Ka'ba in Makka is a *Haram*, and the area around the Prophet's Mosque in Madina is a *Haram*. They are referred to together as *al-Haramayn*, 'the two *Harams*'.

Harun: Aaron.

Hawwa: Eve.

hawa: passion, desire.

Hijra: emigration for the Cause of Allah, especially designating the emigration of the Prophet from Makka to Madina.

Ibrahim: Abraham.

ihram: the conditions of clothing and behaviour adopted by someone on *hajj* or *'umra*.

ihsan: absolute sincerity to Allah in oneself, to worship Allah as if you were seeing Him because He sees you.

ikhlas: the state of being absolutely sincere to Allah.

insan: a human being.

'Isa: Jesus.

'Isha': the Night Prayer.

Is'haq:	Isaac.
Isma'il:	Ishmael.
Isra/mi'raj:	the Night Journey of the Prophet ﷺ from Makka to Jerusalem and thence through the seven heavens to the Divine Presence.
Israfil:	The angel charged with blowing the horn that ends the universe.
jamra (jamrat):	the pillars stoned by the pilgrims during the *hajj*.
Jibril:	Gabriel.
jihad:	struggle, particularly fighting in the Cause of Allah to establish and defend Islam.
jizya:	a tax imposed on non-Muslims under the protection of Muslim rule.
Khilafa:	the caliphate.
Khalifa:	the khalif or caliph.
kufr:	unbelief, rejection of Allah, also ingratitude.
Laylatu'l-Qadr:	"the Night of Power" mentioned in *sura* 97 of the Qur'an.
Lut:	Lot.
ma'rifa:	gnosis, direct knowledge of Allah.
Maryam:	Mary.
Maghrib:	the Sunset Prayer.
Masjid al-Haram:	the great mosque in Makka. The Ka'ba is situated in it.
Mika'il:	Michael.
miqat:	one of the designated places for entering into *ihram* for *hajj* or *'umra*.
Mizan:	balance, scale.
Muhajirun:	Companions of the Messenger of Allah who accepted Islam in Makka and emigrated to Madina.
mujahidun:	those doing *jihad*.

Musa:	Moses.
nafs:	the self, usually in reference to the lower self.
nisab:	minimum amount of wealth on which *zakat* is due.
Nuh:	Noah.
qasas:	story, narrative aspects of the Qur'an.
qibla:	the direction faced in the prayer, which is towards the Ka'ba in Makka.
rak'at:	a unit of the prayer consisting of a series of standings, bowing, prostrations and sittings.
ruku':	bowing, particularly the bowing position in the prayer.
sa':	measure of volume equal to four *mudds*, a *mudd* being a double-handed scoop.
sa'y:	a rite of *'umra* and *hajj*. It consists of going seven times between the hills of Safa and Marwa, adjacent to the Ka'ba.
sadaqa:	giving for the sake of Allah, a charitable gift without any ulterior motive.
sajda:	prostration.
sakina:	an enveloping stillness which Allah sends down on the heart.
Salaf:	the early generations of the Muslims.
salam:	the greeting '*as-Salamu 'alaykum*'. It terminates the prayer.
salat:	the daily prayers.
sawm:	fasting.
shahada(tayn):	bearing witness, particularly witnessing that there is no god but Allah and that Muhammad is the Messenger of Allah.
shahawat:	physical appetites.
Shari'a:	the legal structure of a people based on the revelation received or followed by their Prophet. The final *Shari'a* is that of Islam.

Shaytan, pl. **shayateen**: a devil, particularly Iblis.

shirk: the grave wrong action of worshipping something or someone other than Allah or associating something or someone as a partner with Him.

sira: 'conduct, behaviour, way of acting', hence a biography, particularly the biography of the Prophet ﷺ.

Sirat: the narrow bridge which spans the Fire and must be crossed to enter the Garden. It is described as sharper than a sword and thinner than a hair.

Subh: the Dawn Prayer.

suhur: the early morning meal taken before first light when fasting.

sujud: prostration.

Sunna: the customary practice of a person or group of people. It has come to refer almost exclusively to the practice of the Messenger of Allah.

sura: chapter of the Qur'an.

takbir: saying '*Allahu Akbar*', "Allah is greater".

takbir al-ihram: the *takbir* which begins the prayer.

talbiya: saying '*Labbayk*', "At Your service" during the *hajj*.

taqwa: awe or fear of Allah, which inspires a person to guard against doing wrong and eager to do actions which please Him.

tarawih: the night prayers performed in the month of Ramadan.

tasawwuf: Sufism, the Islamic science of attaining *ihsan* or spiritual excellence.

tasbih: glorification of Allah.

tashahhud: to pronounce the *shahada*. In the context of the prayer, it is a formula which includes the *shahada* and is said in the sitting position at the end of a two *rak'at* cycle of prayer.

tawaf: circumambulation of the Ka'ba, done in sets of

seven circuits.

tawhid:	the doctrine of Divine Unity.
tayyib:	wholesome.
'umra:	the lesser pilgrimage to the Ka'ba in Makka performed at any time of the year.
umma:	the worldwide community of Muslims.
wasq:	a measure of volume equal to sixty *sa's*.
wudu':	ritual washing of the limbs, performed to be pure for the prayer.
zakat:	a wealth tax, one of the five Pillars of Islam.
zakat al-fitr:	a small obligatory head-tax imposed on every Muslim, who has the means, for himself and his dependants. It is paid once yearly at the end of Ramadan.
Zamzam:	the well in the *Haram* of Makka.

Prayers in the text

Glorious is He and exalted.

Mighty is He and majestic.

The above are said after mention of Allah.

May Allah bless him and grant him peace. Said after mention of the Prophet.

Peace be upon him. Said after mention of the Prophet, one of the Prophets and Messengers, or one of the archangels.

May Allah be pleased with him.

May Allah be pleased with her.

May Allah be pleased with them.

The above are said after mention of any of the Companions of the Prophet.

May Allah have mercy on him. Said after mention of those who have passed away.

The Natural Form of Man